This Coloring Book Belongs To:

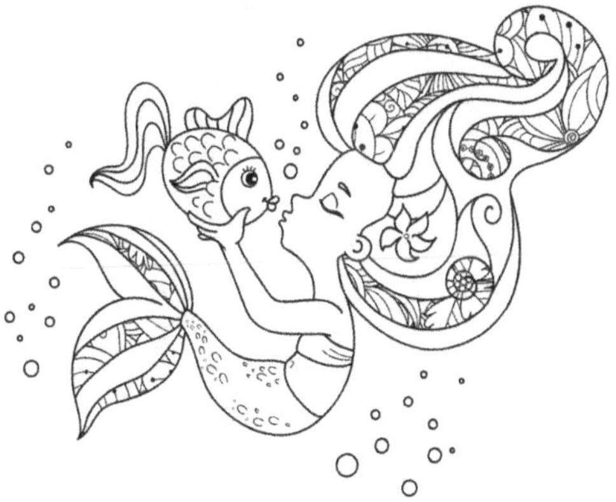

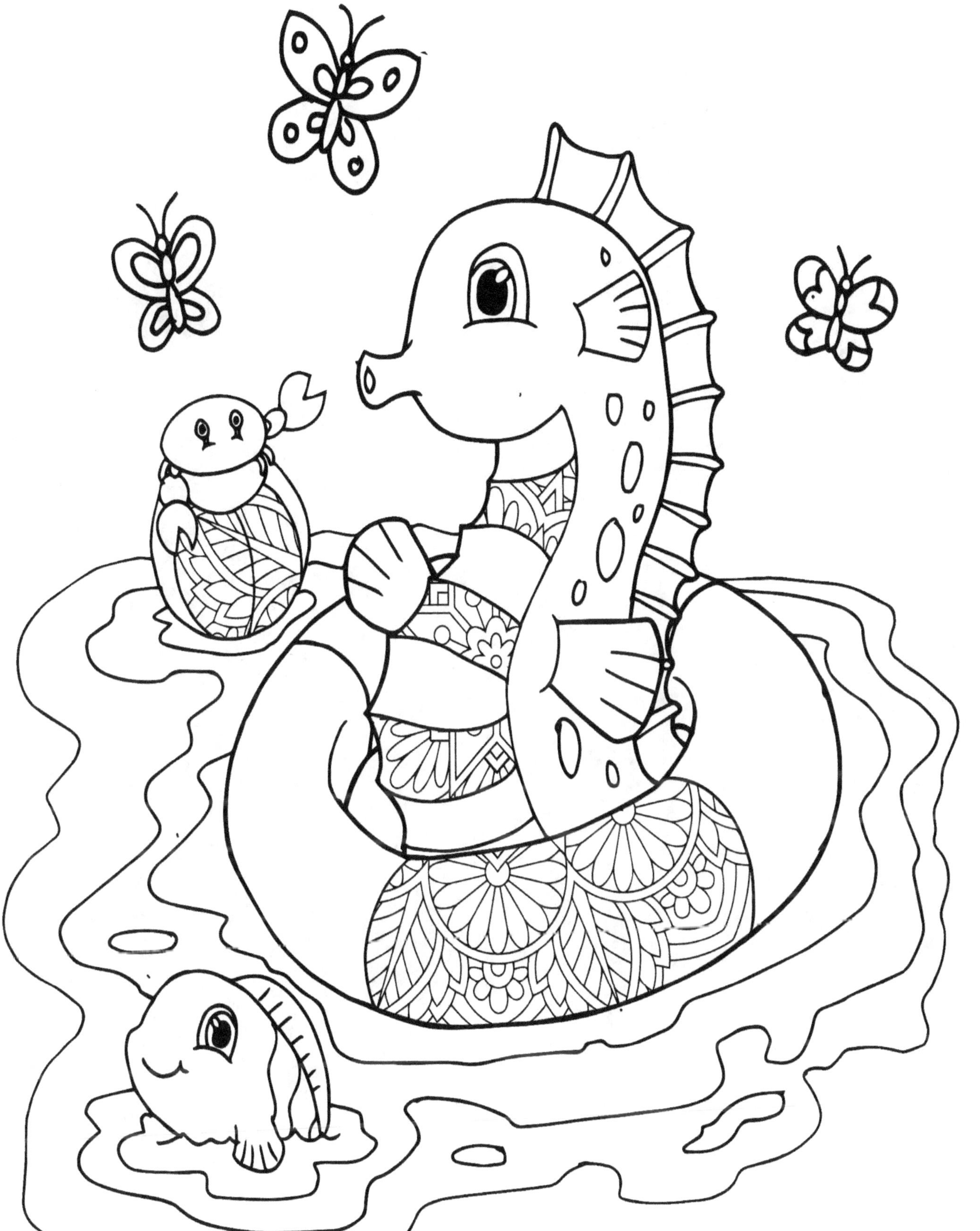

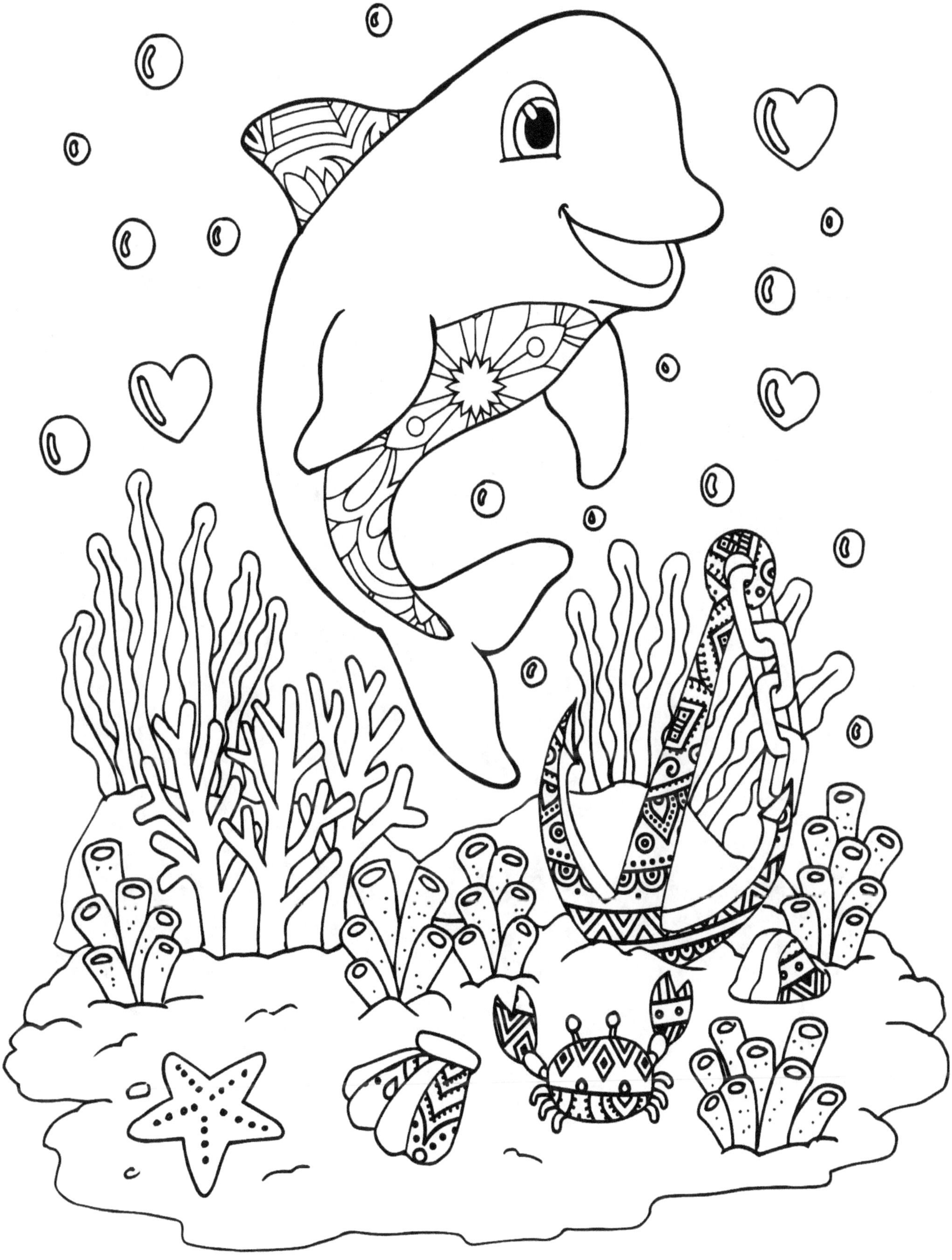

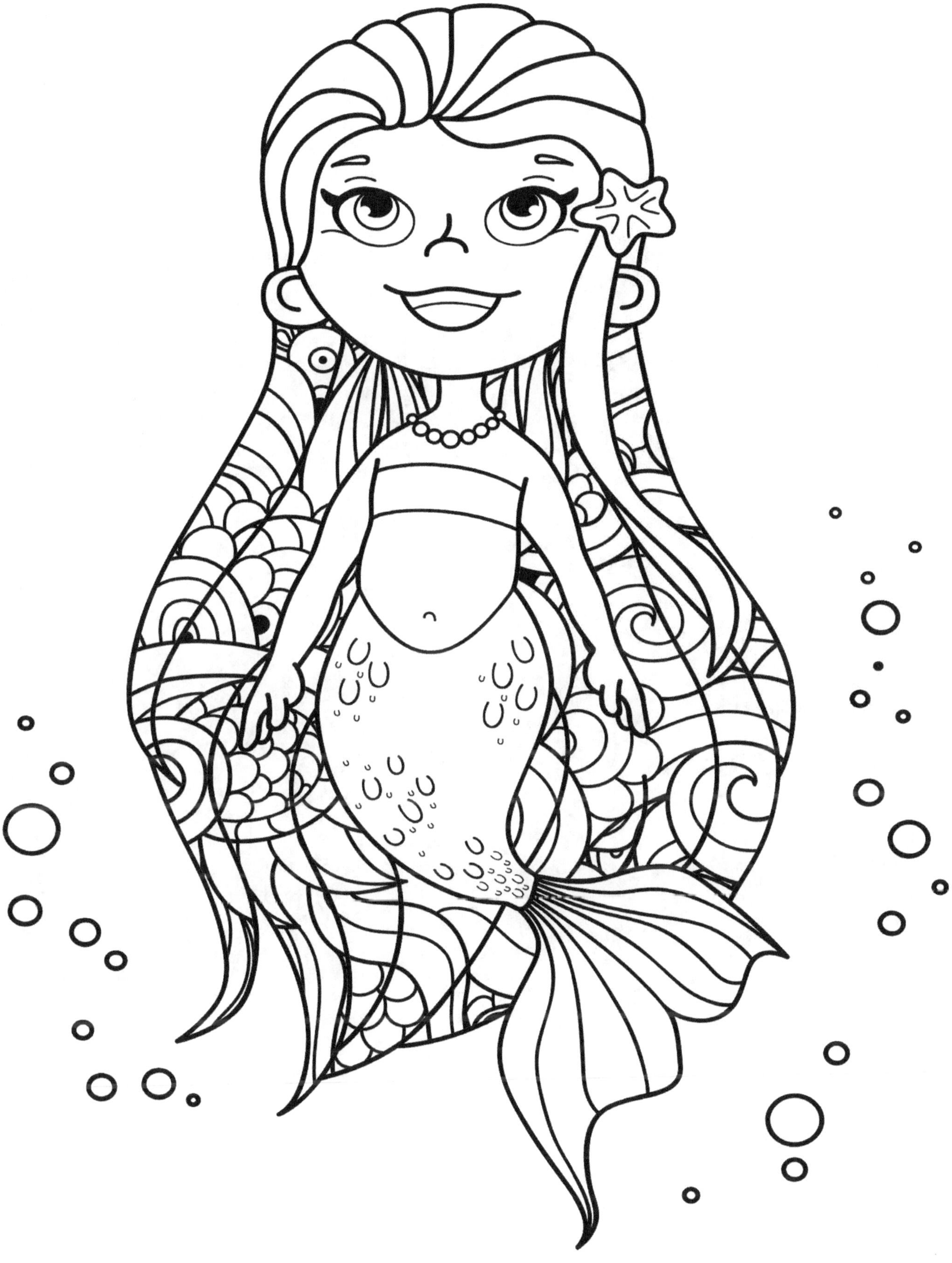

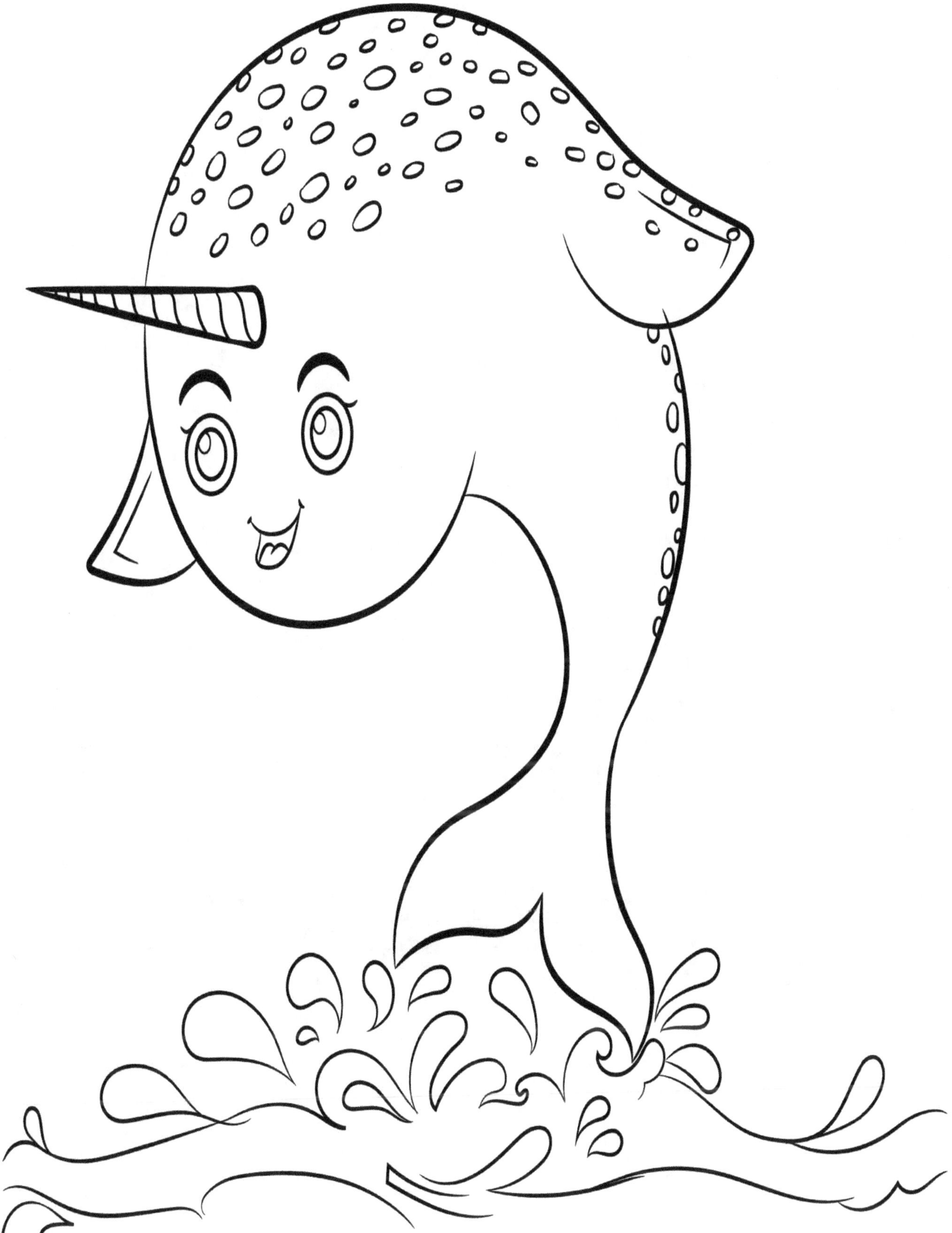

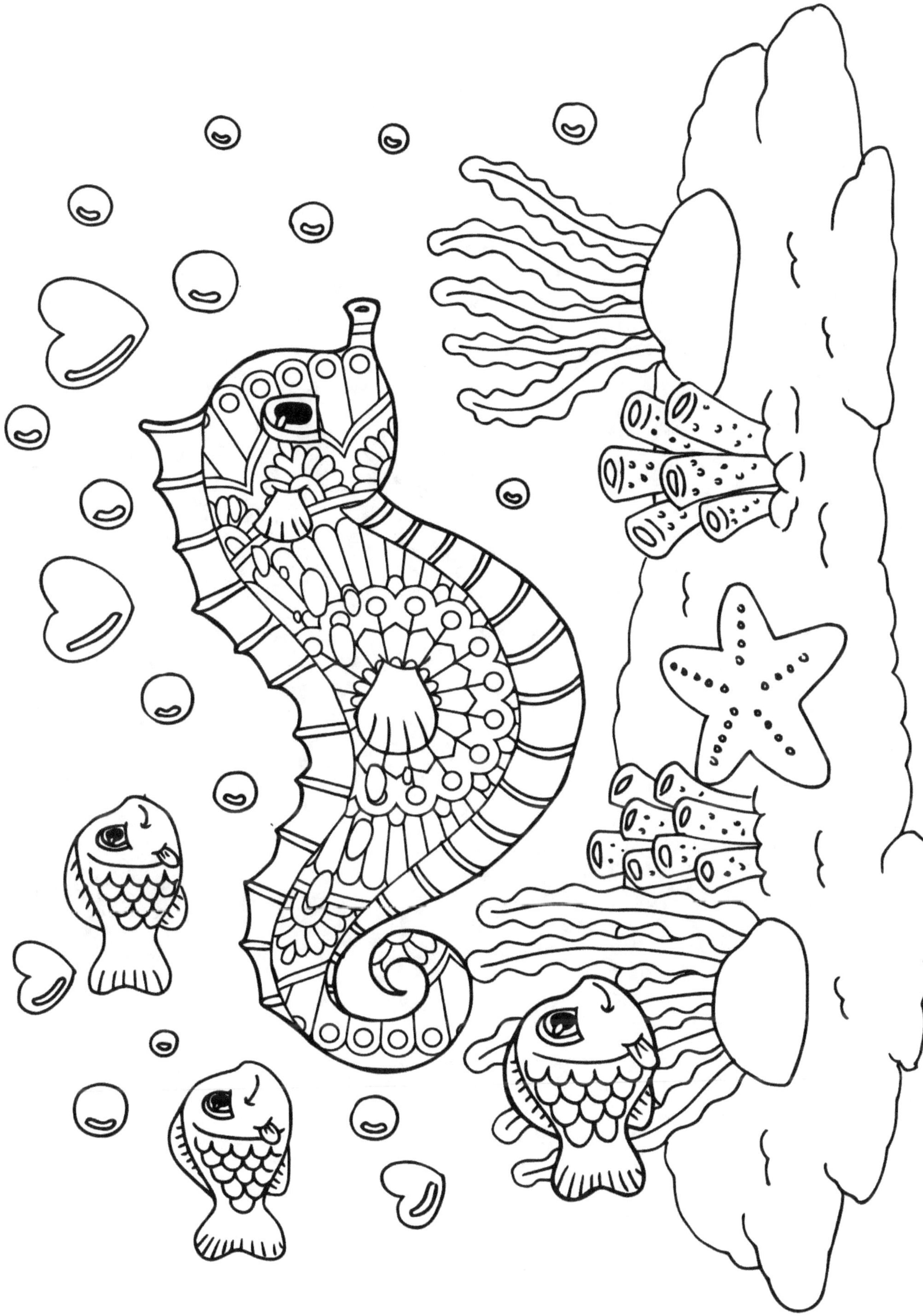

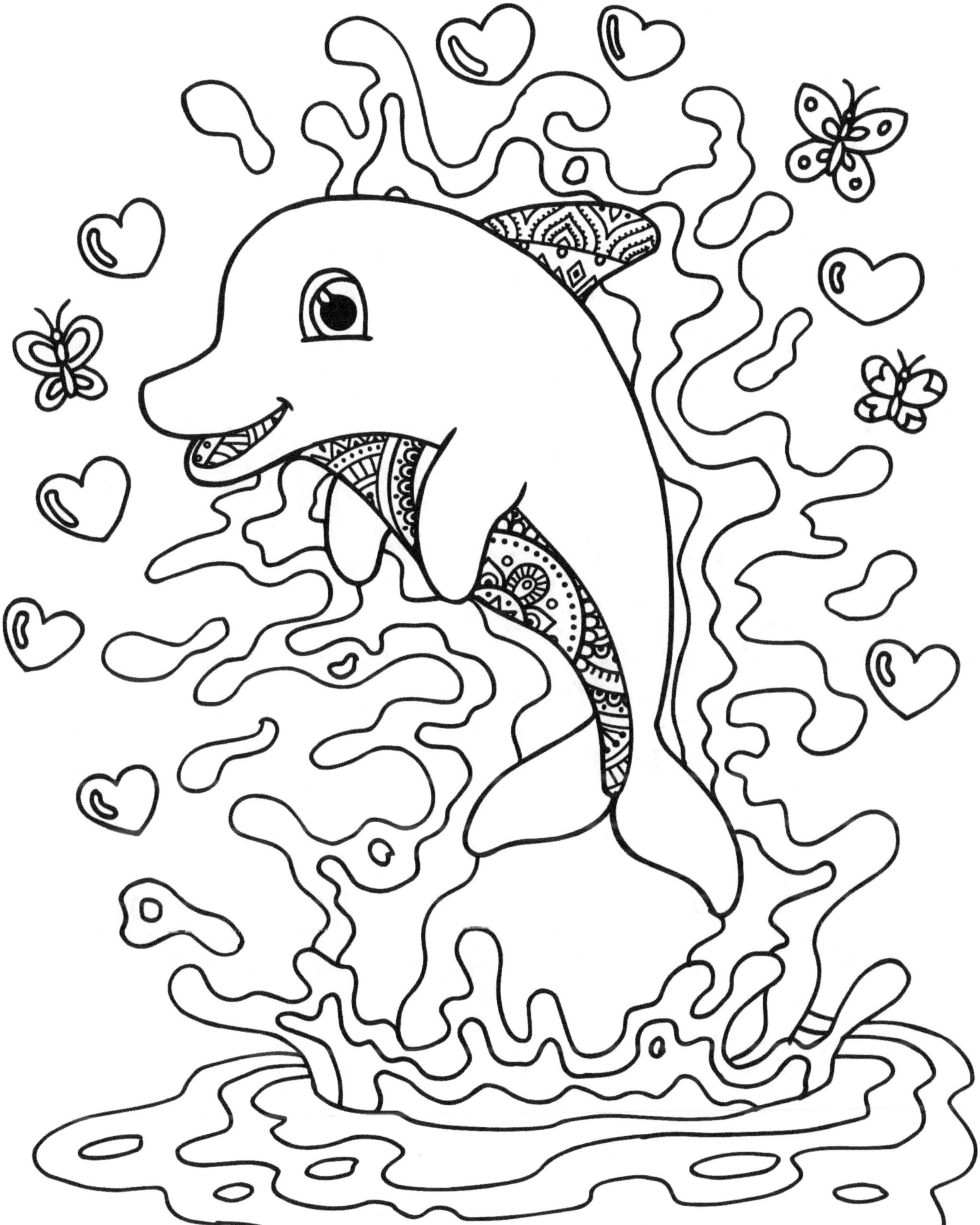

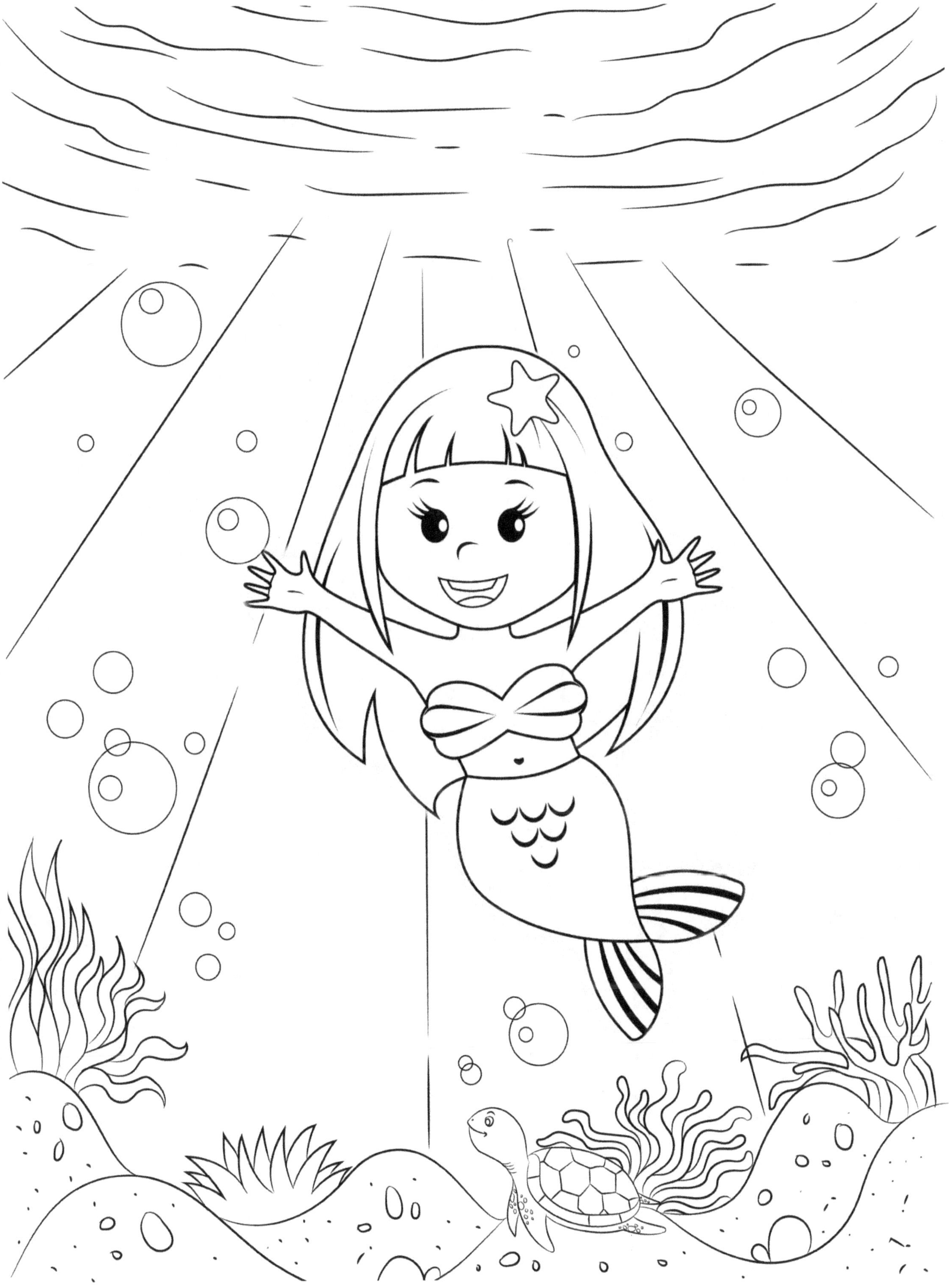

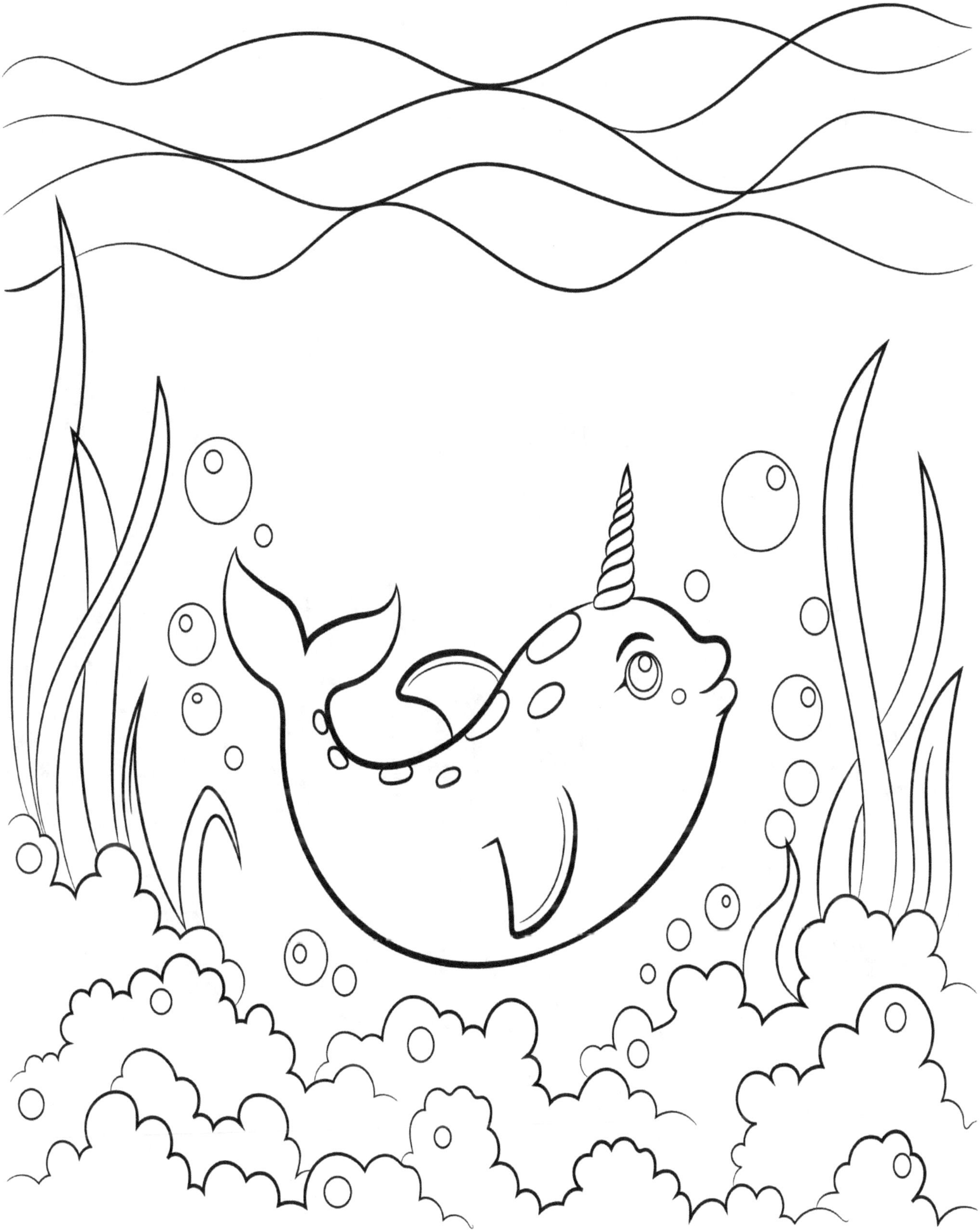

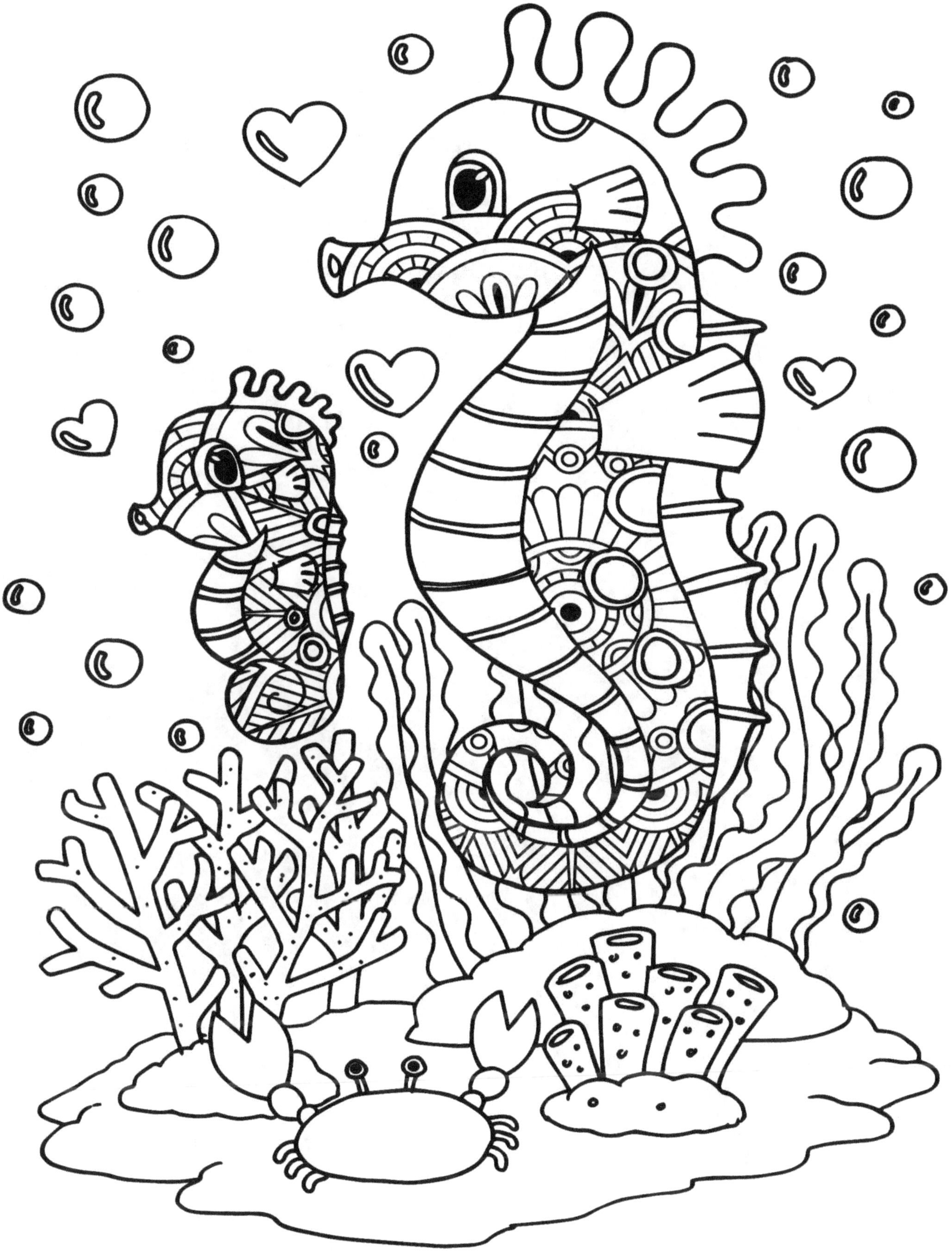

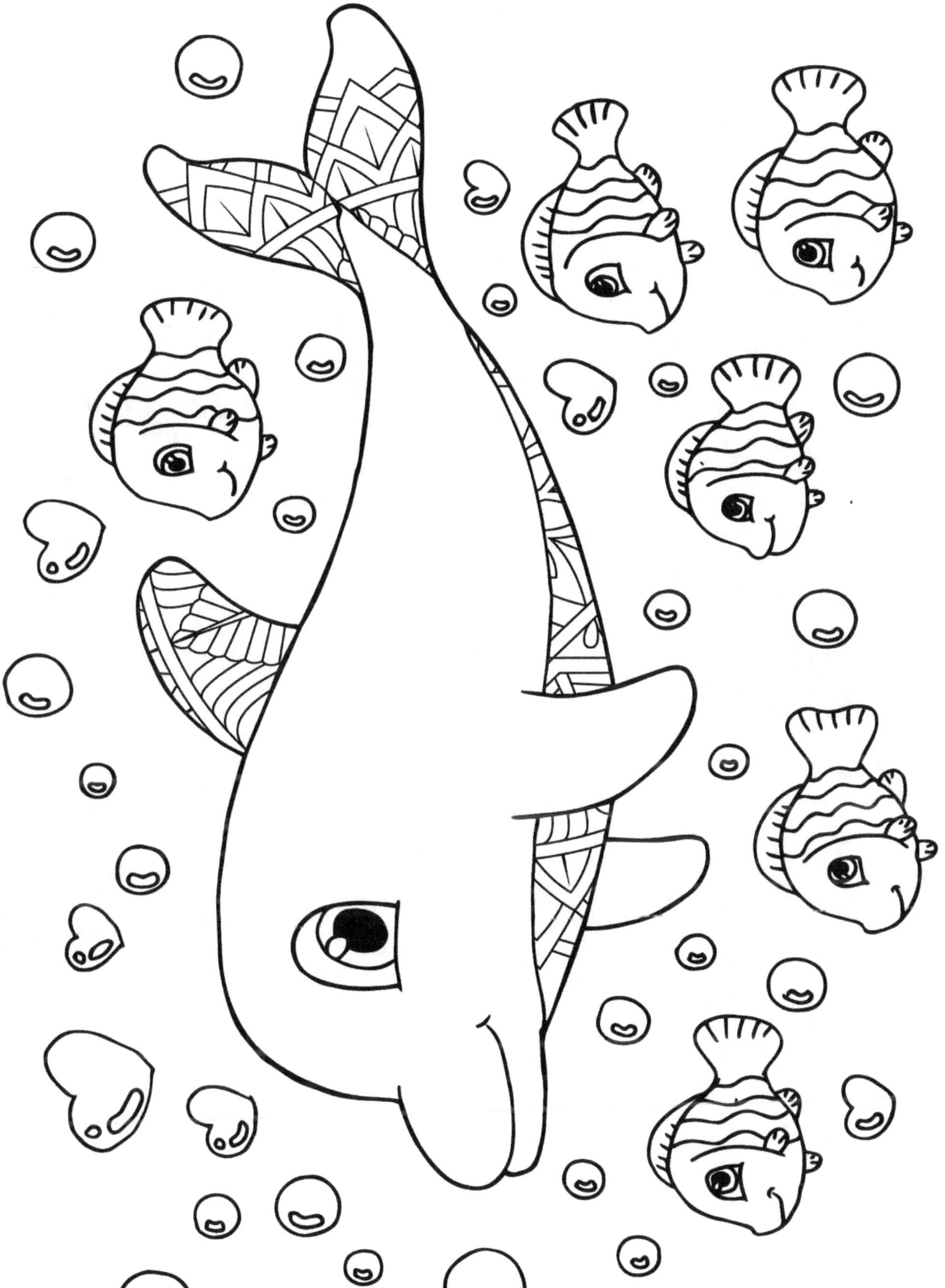

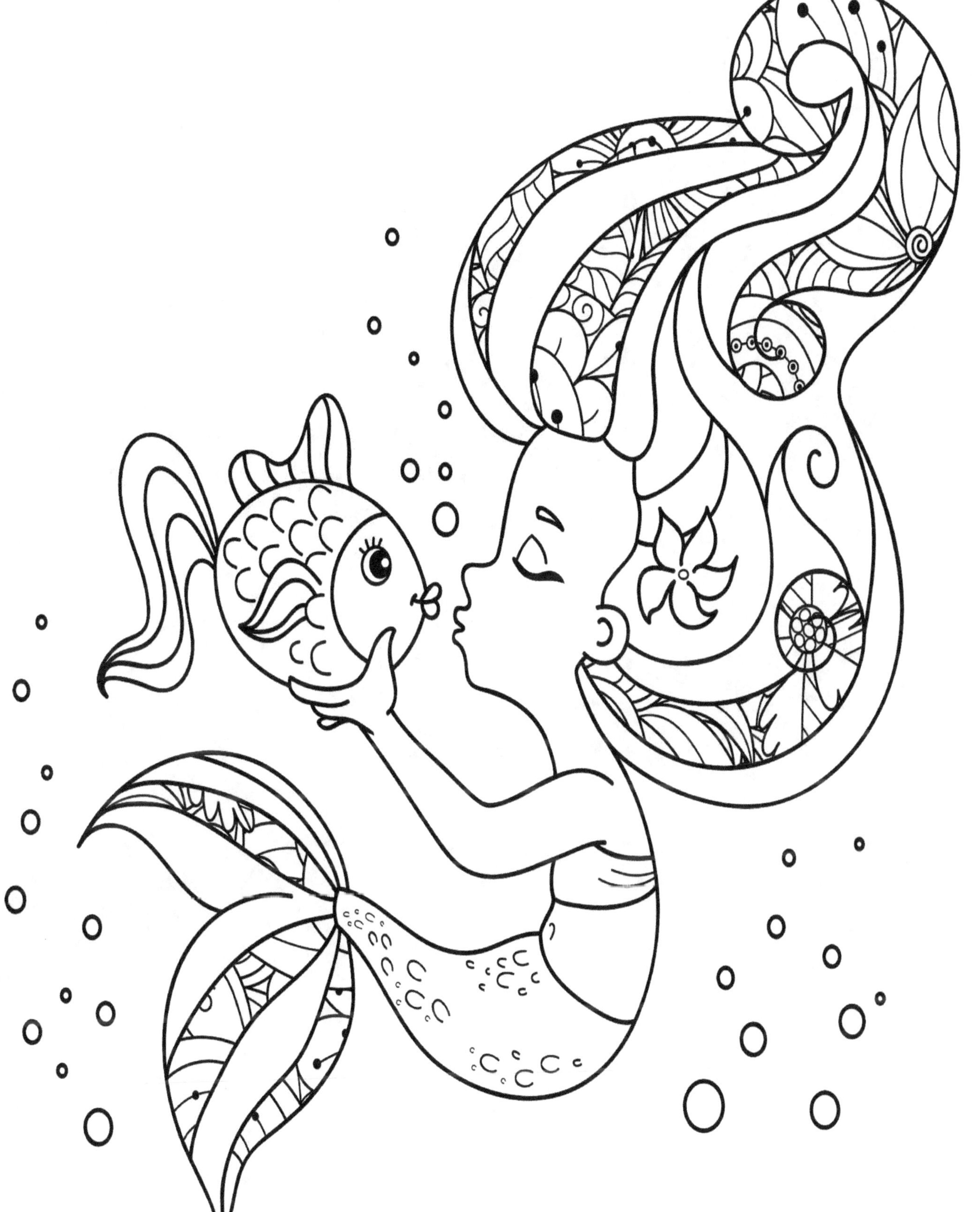

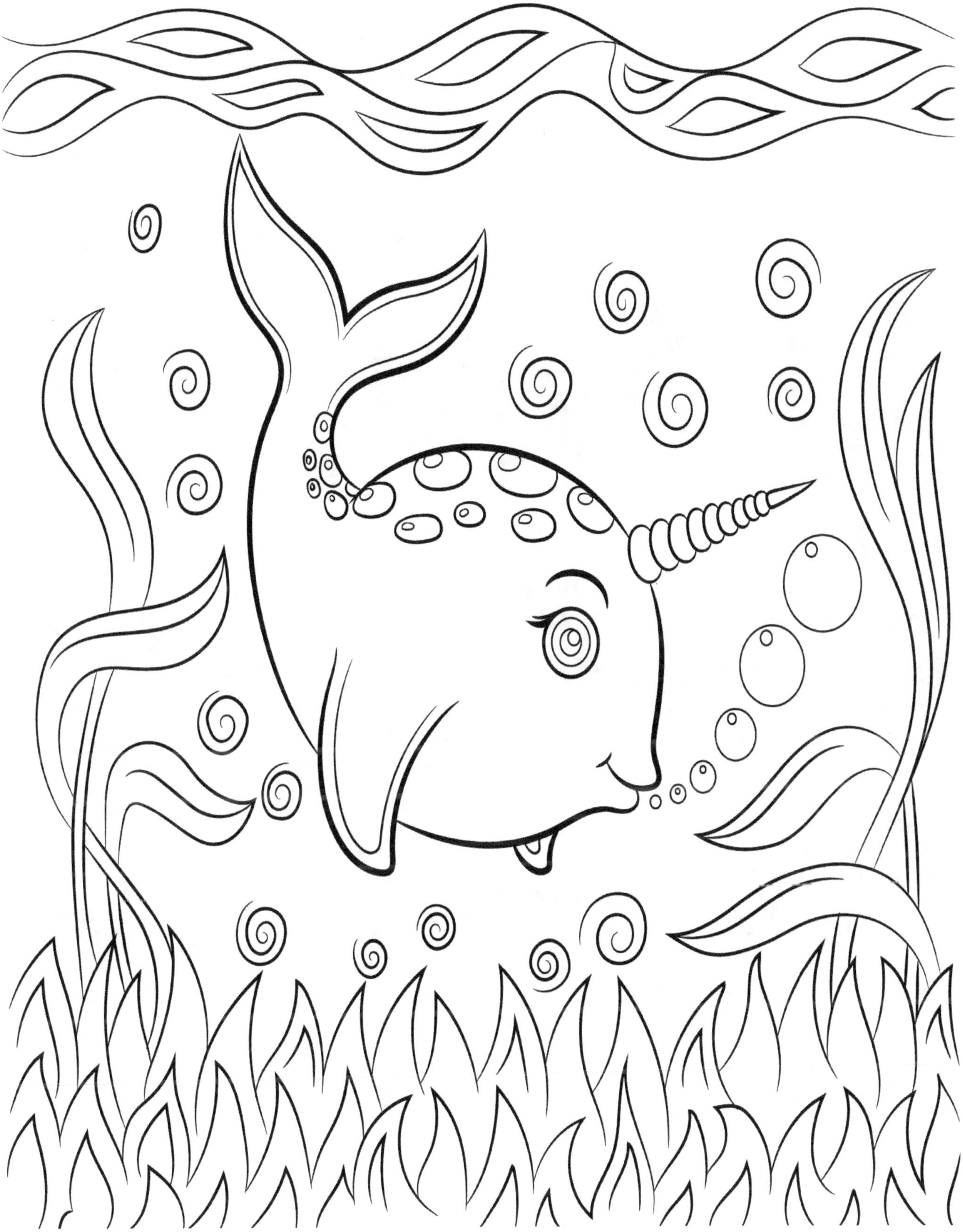

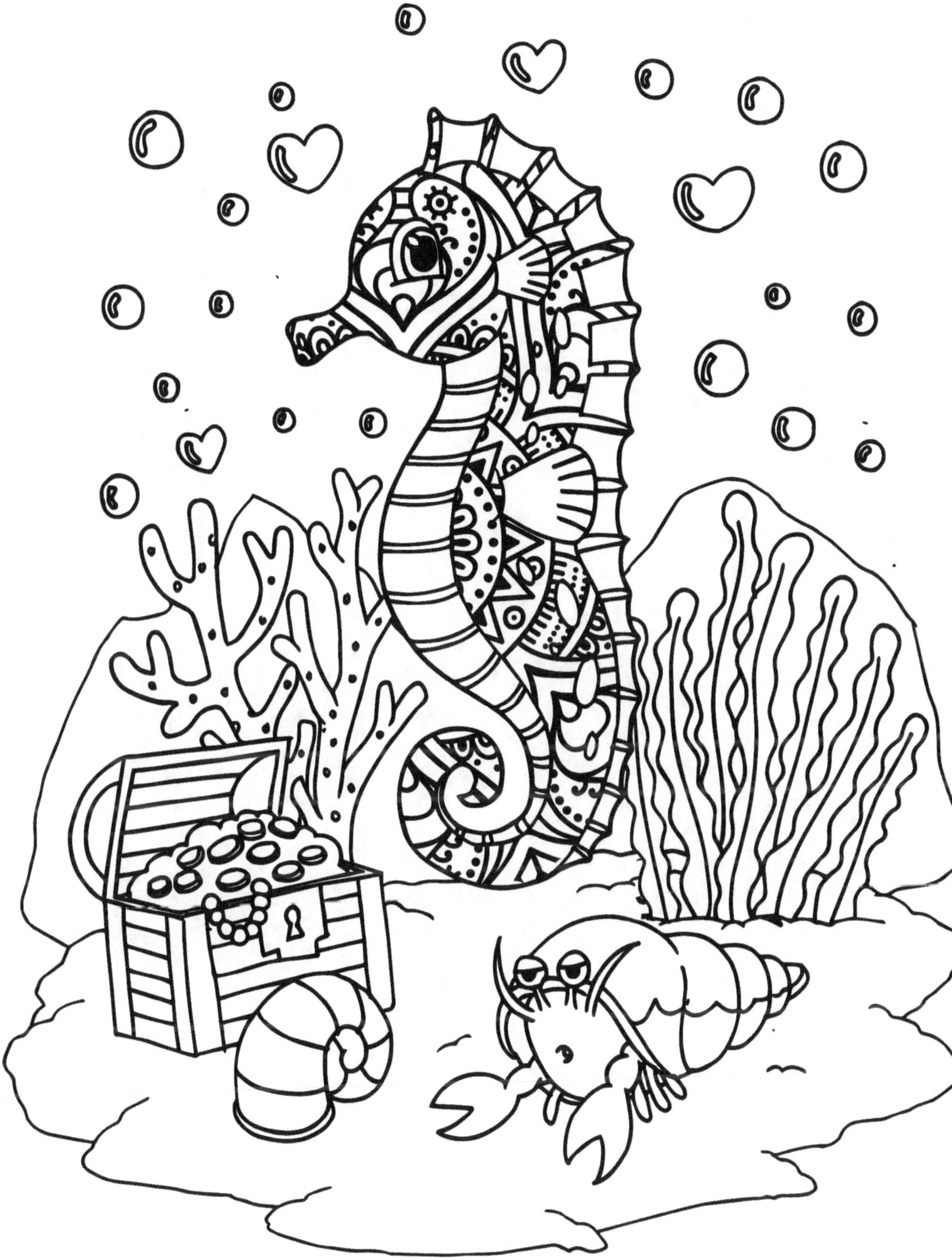

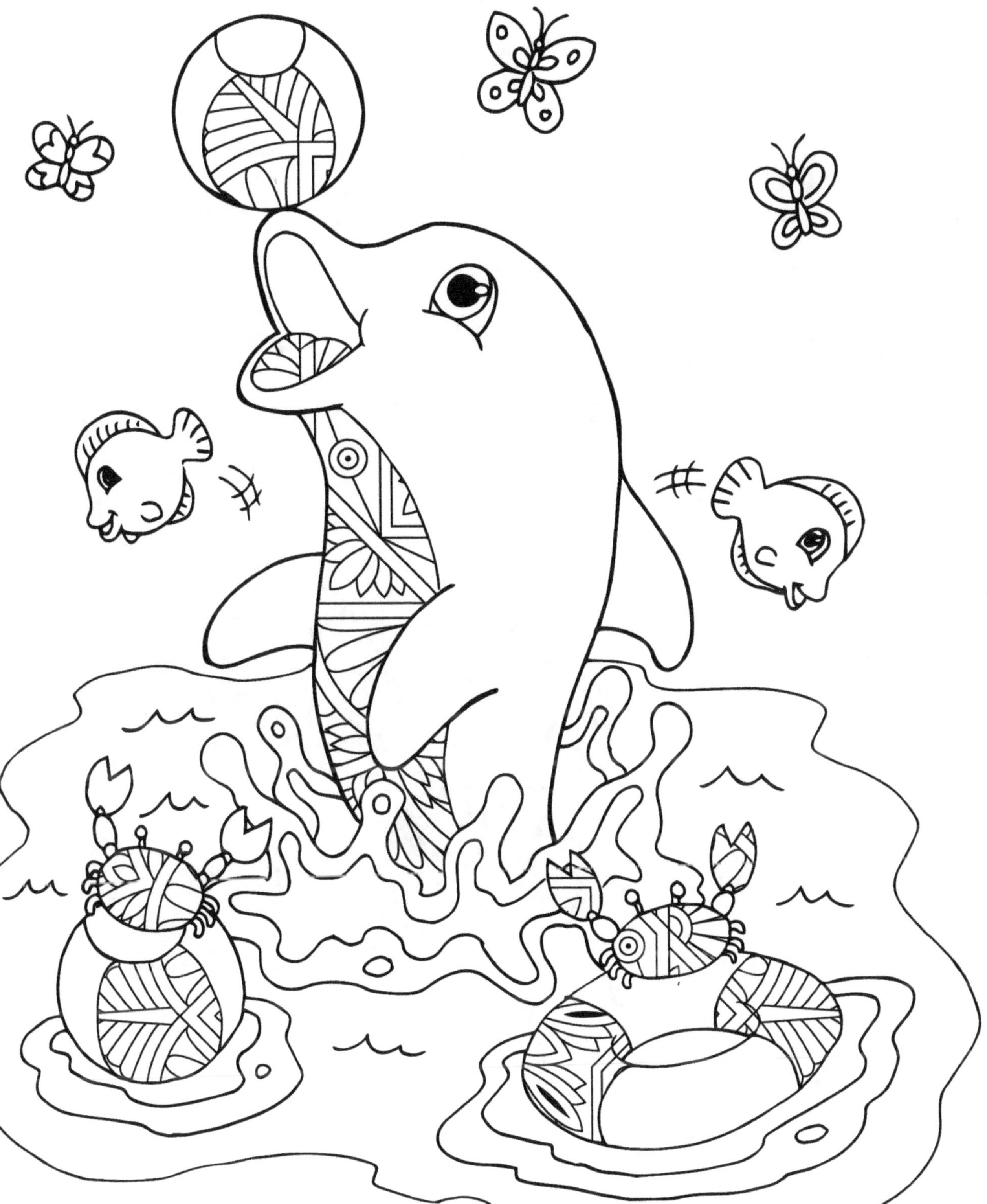

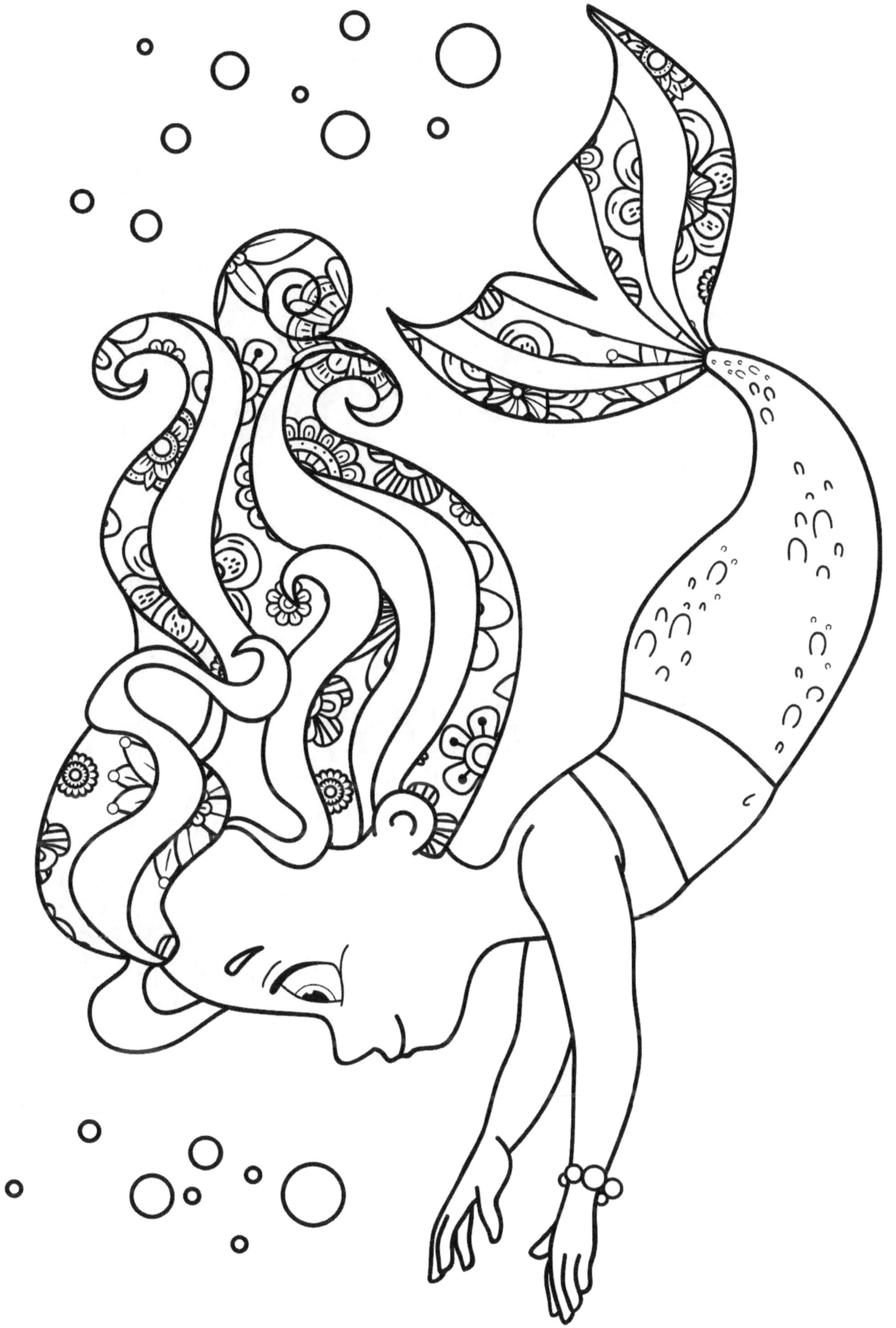

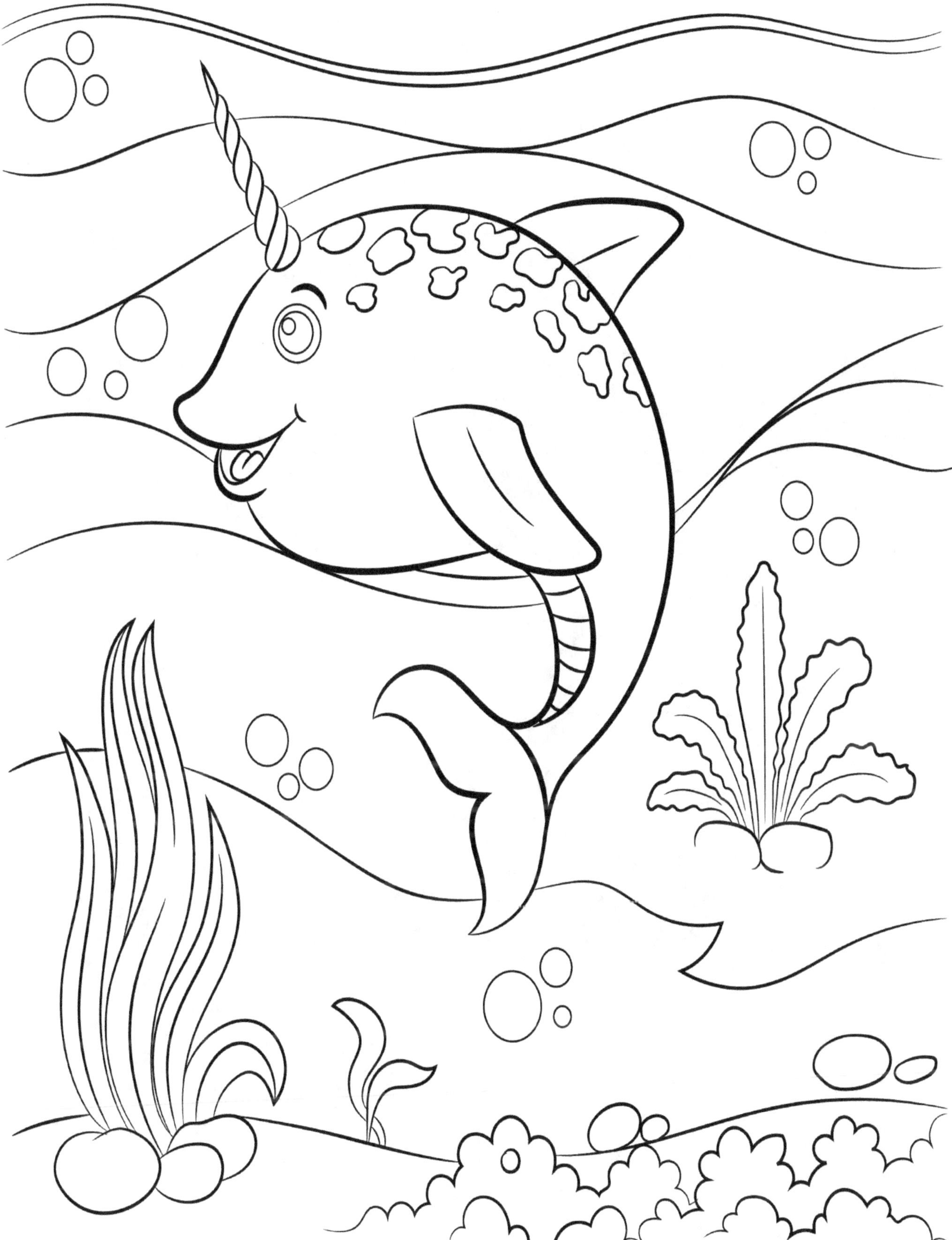

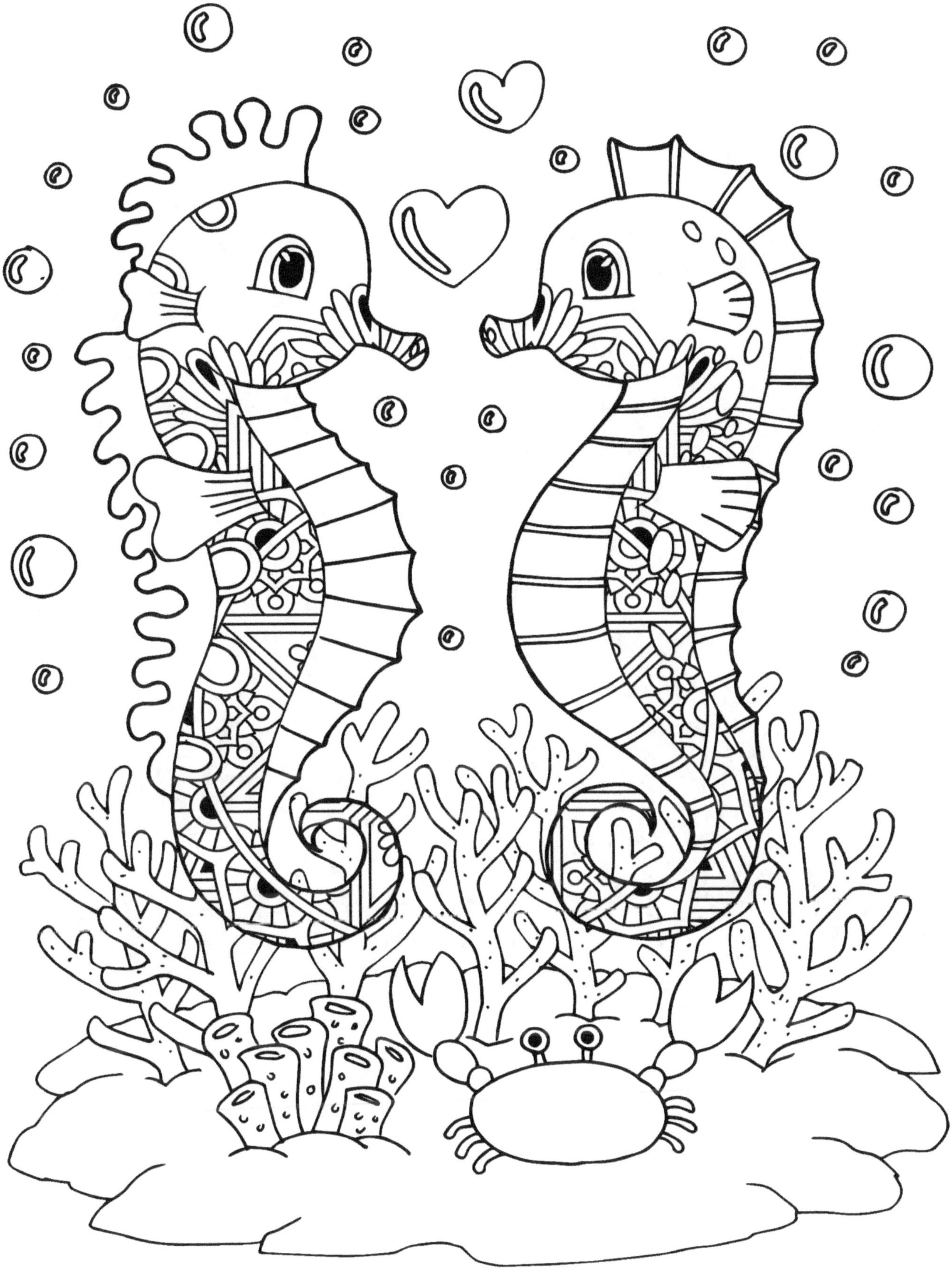

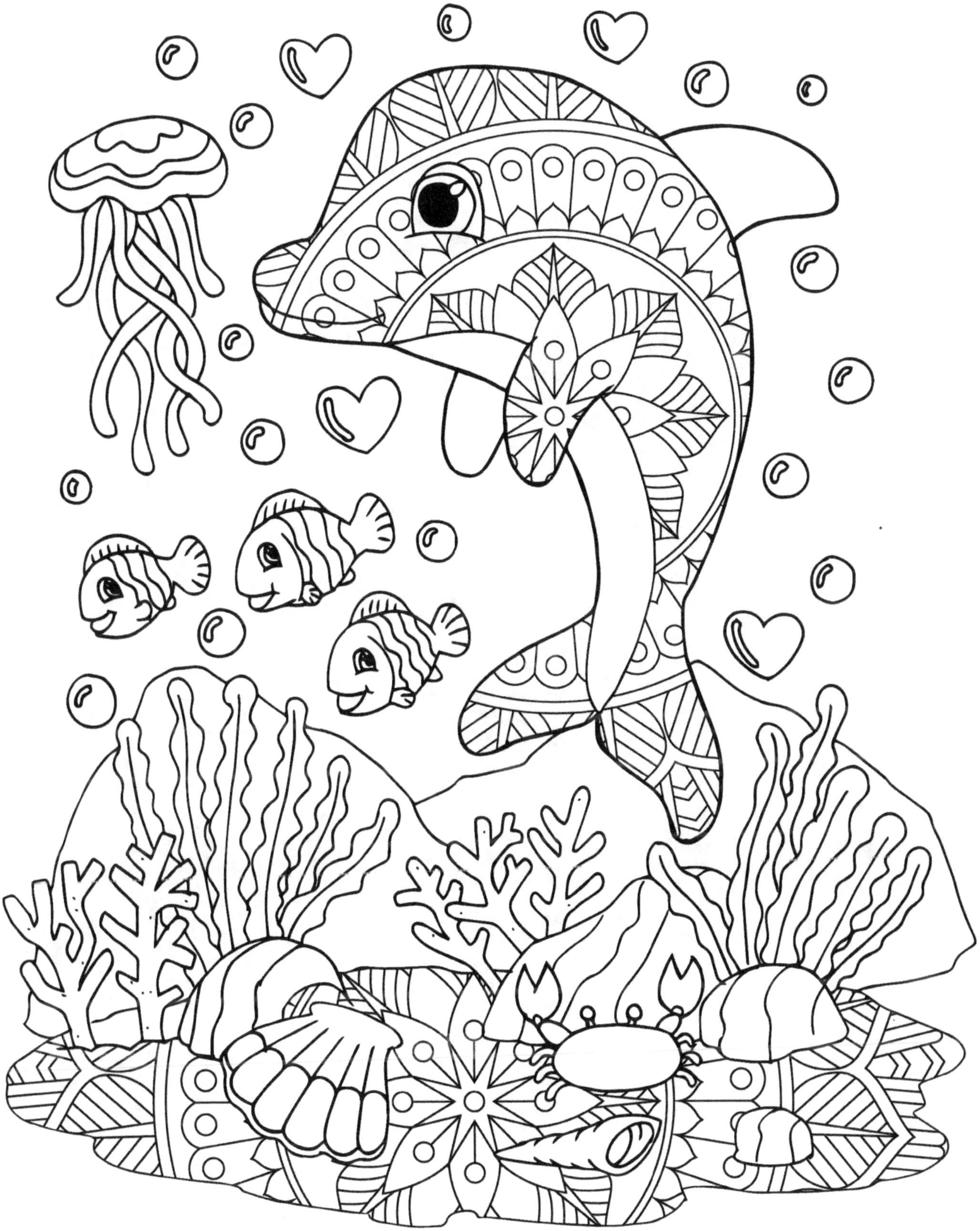

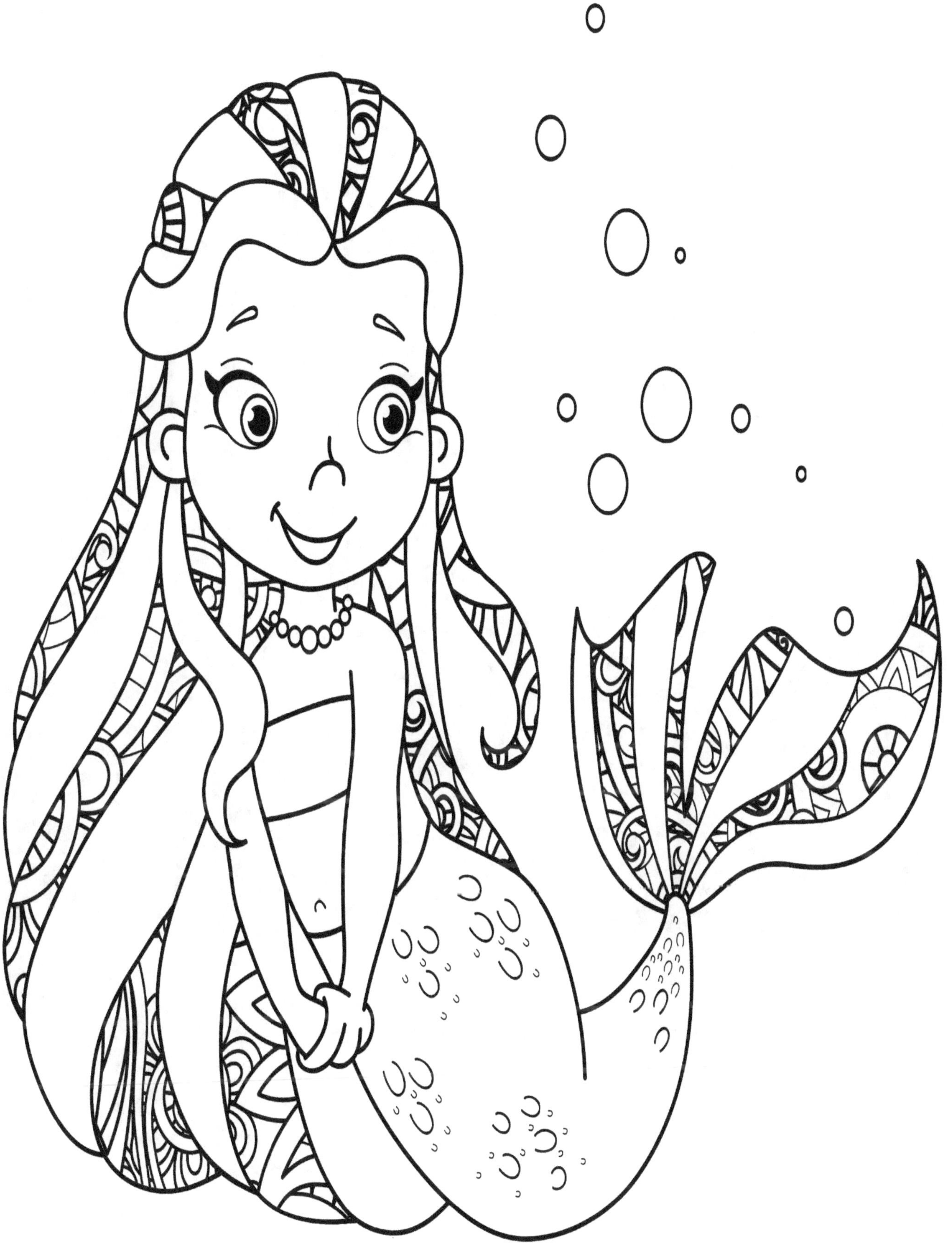

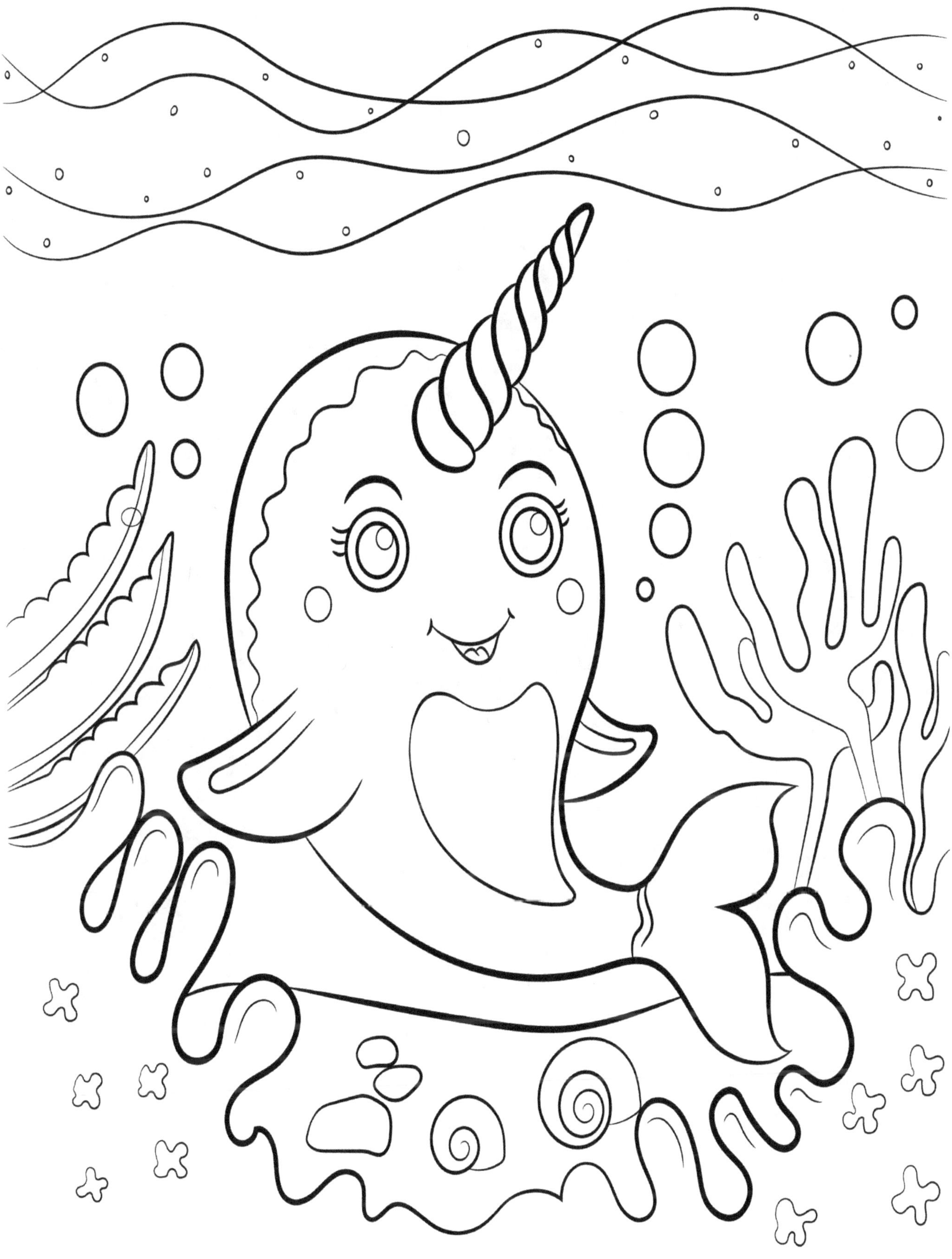

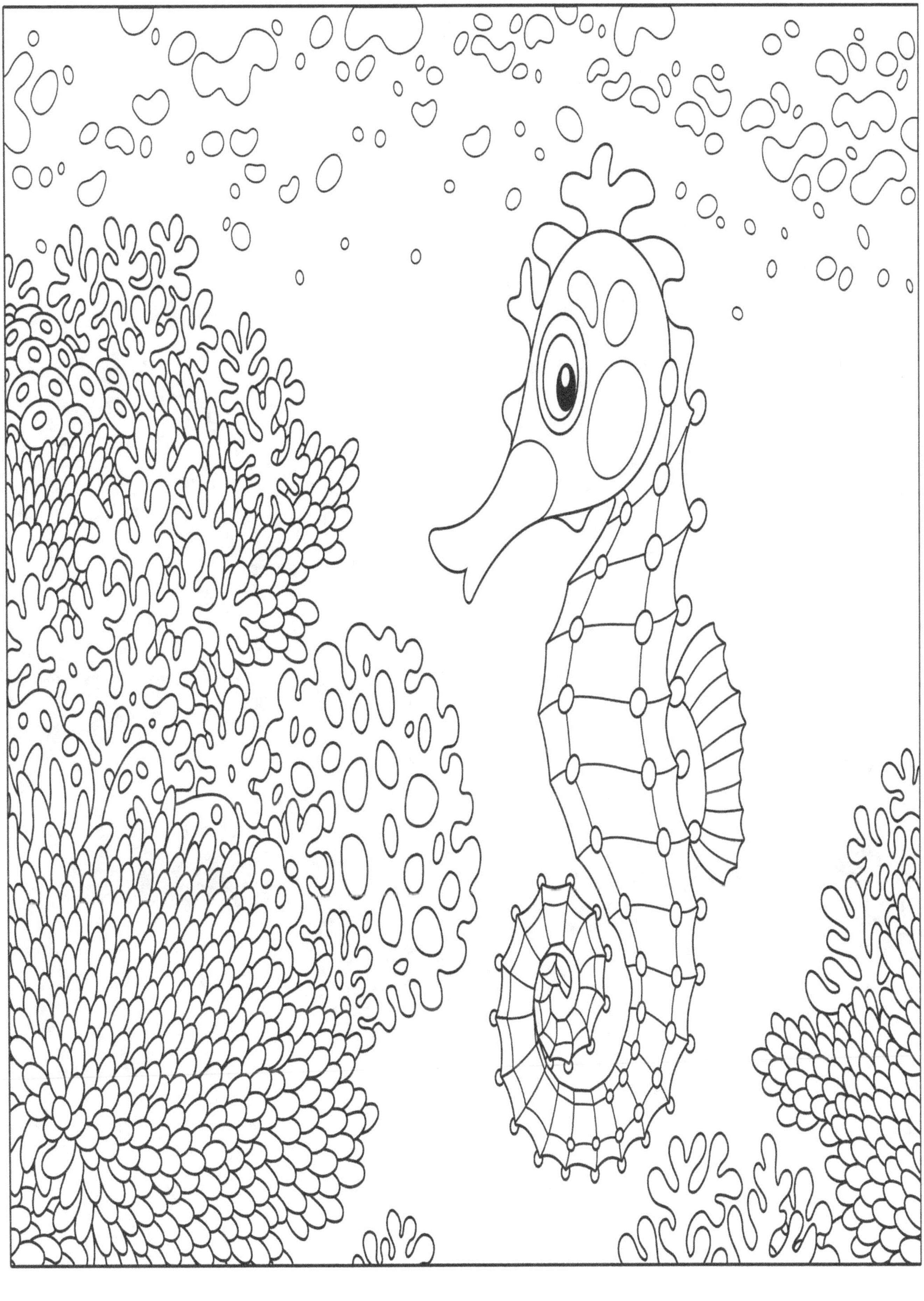

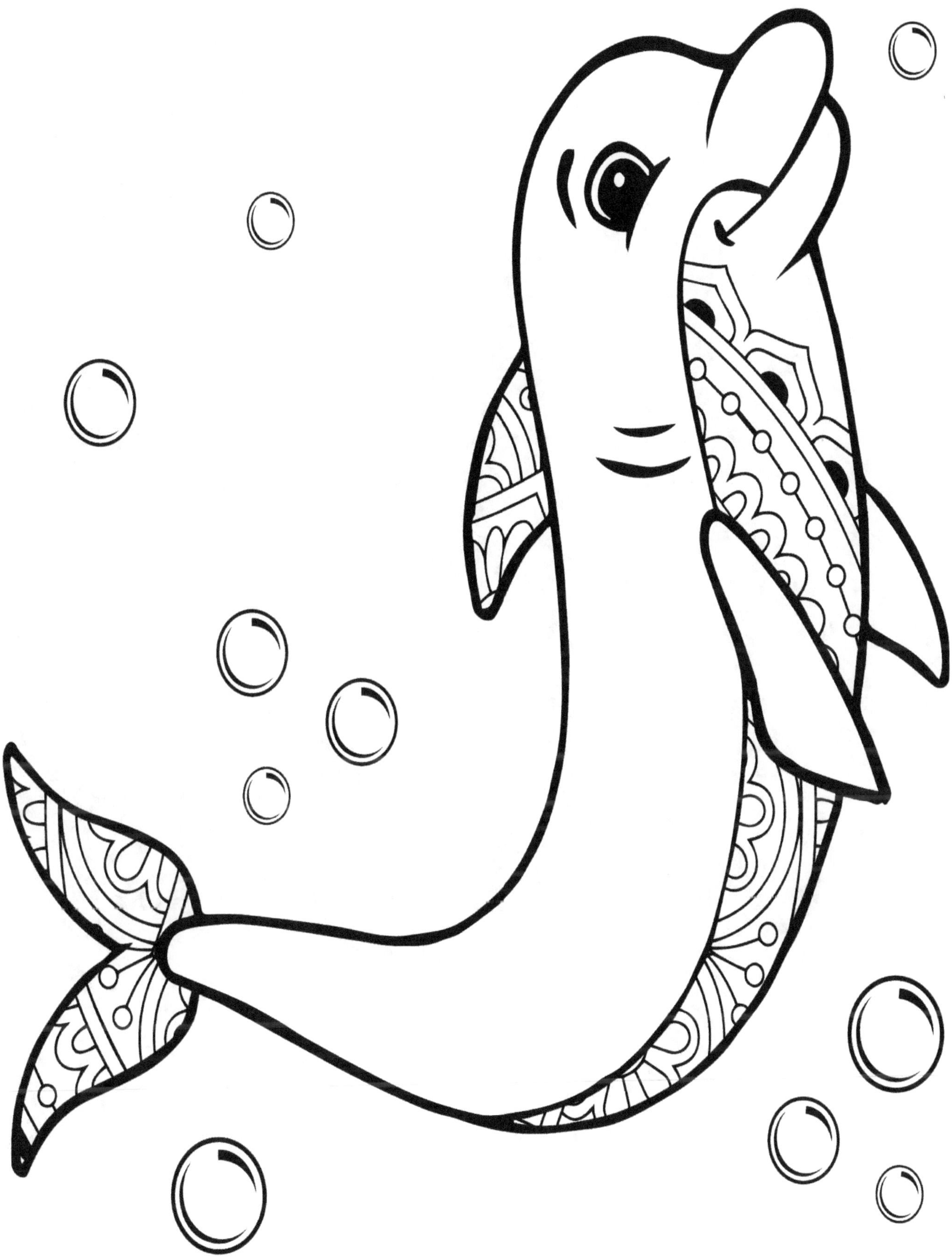

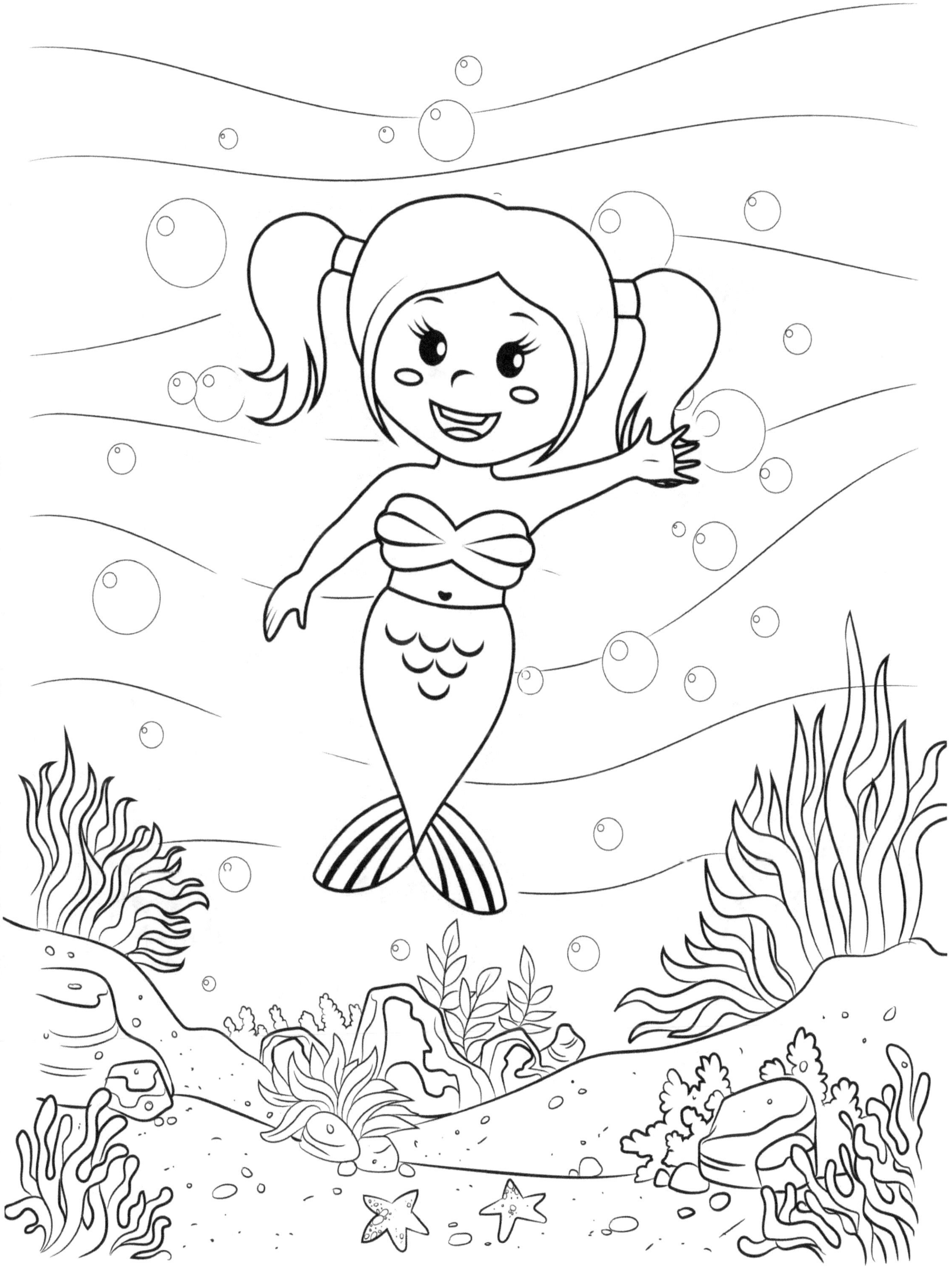

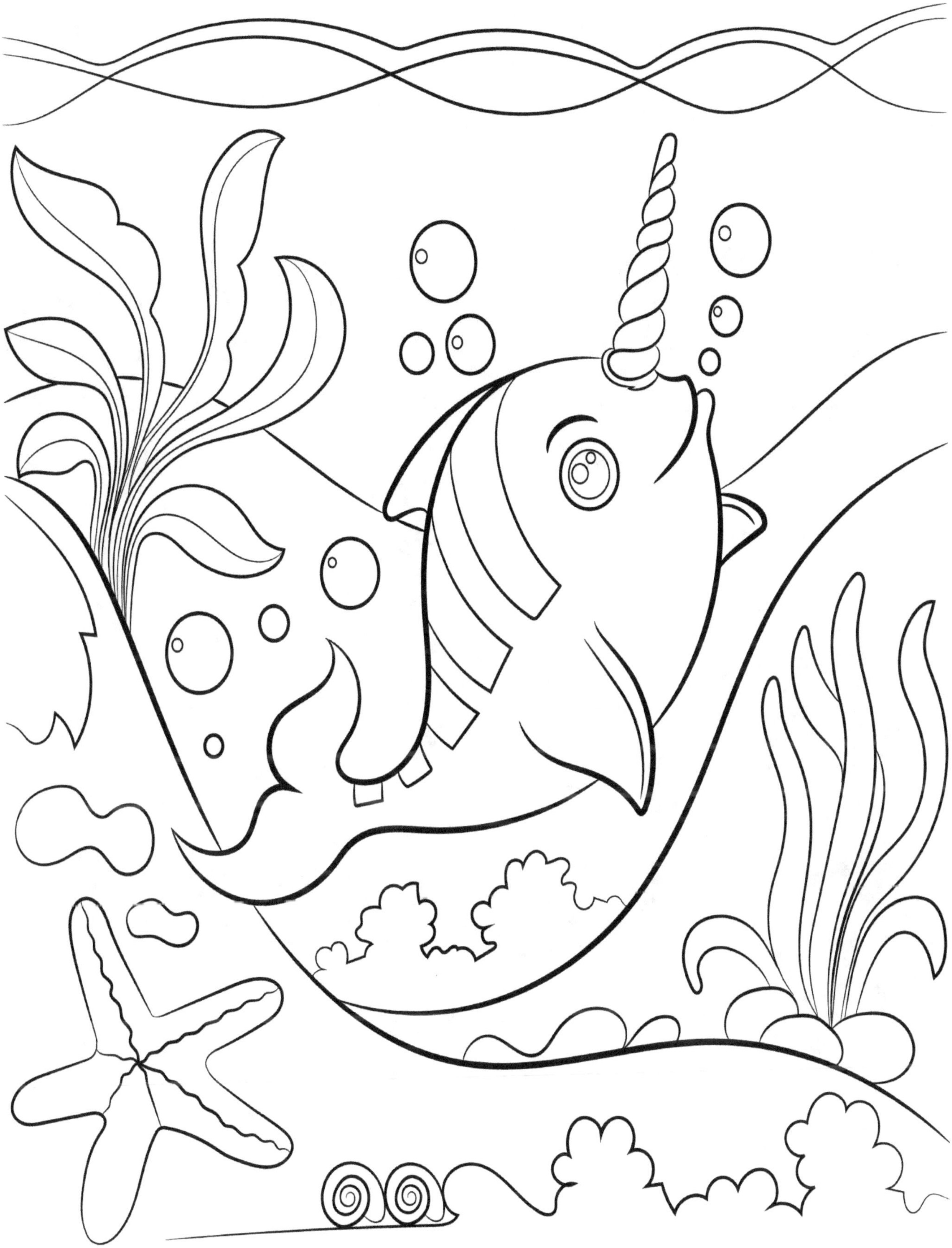

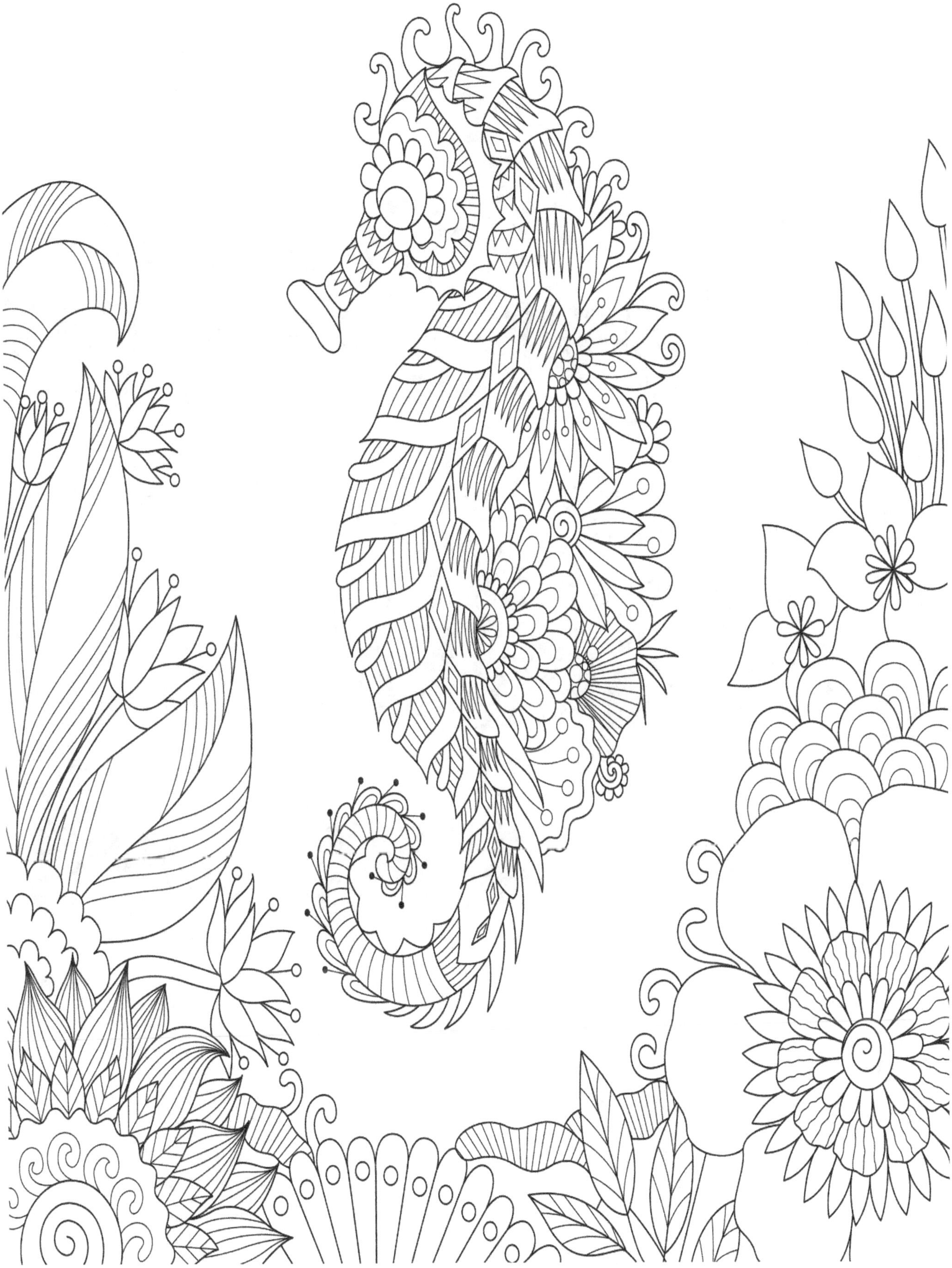

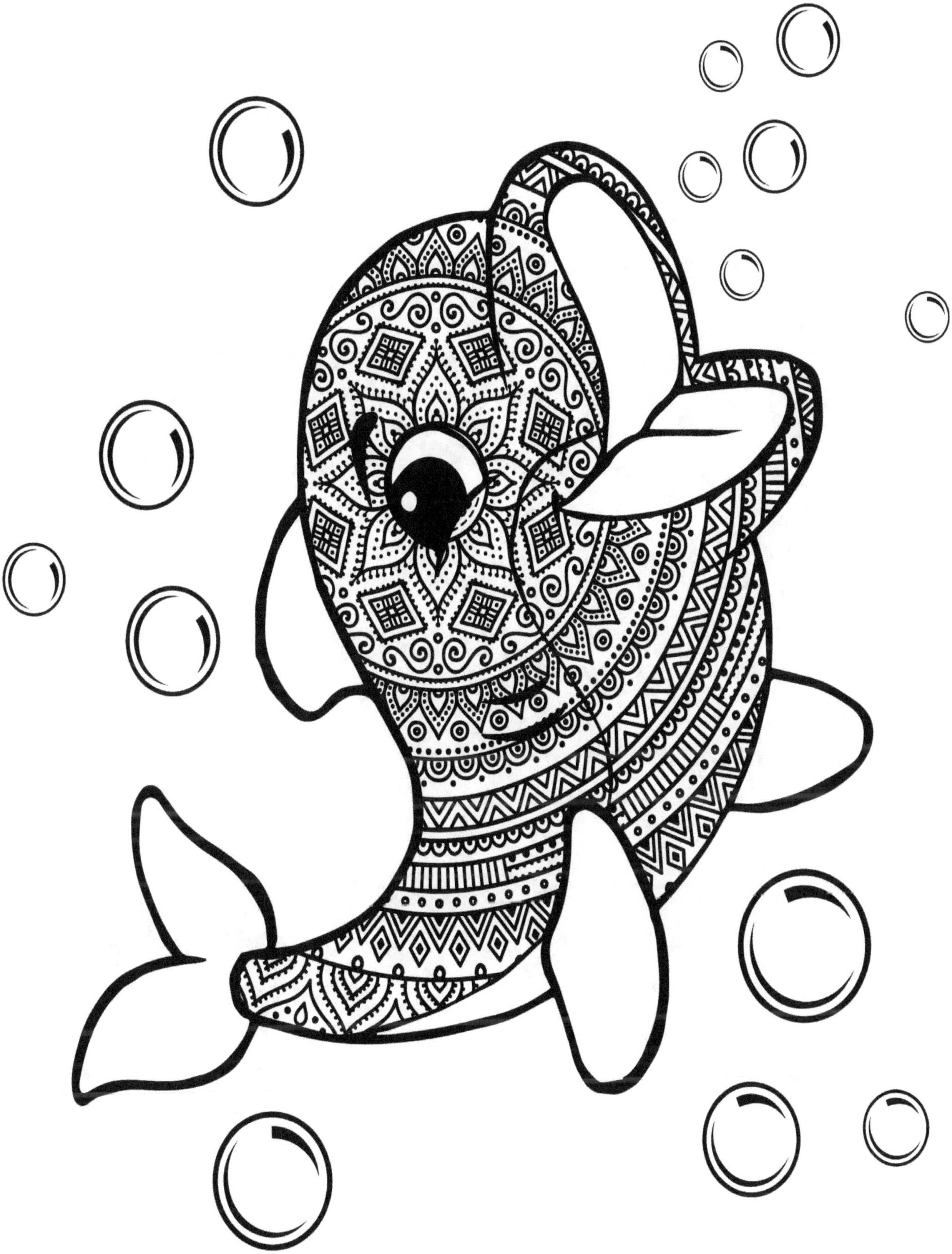

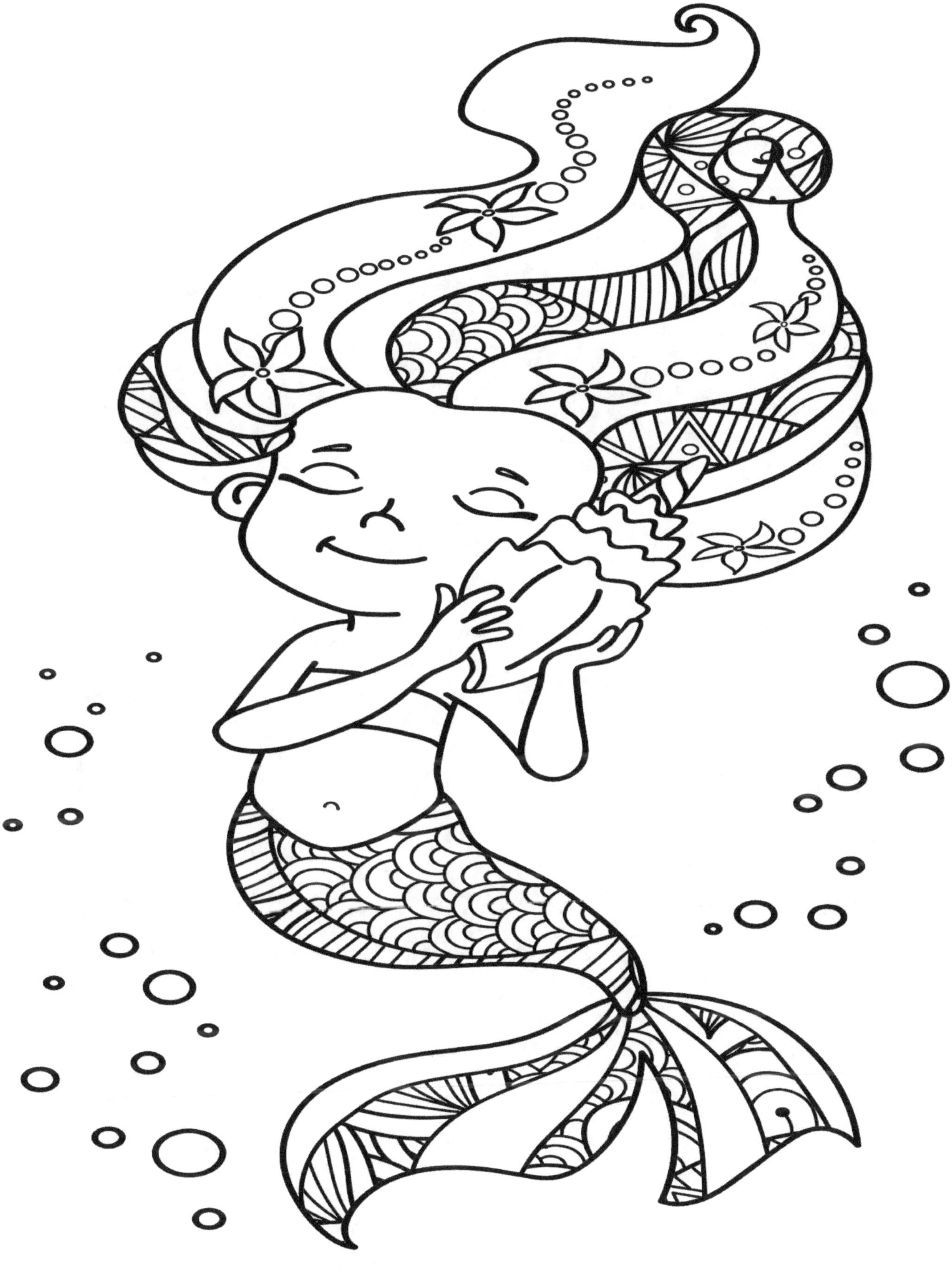

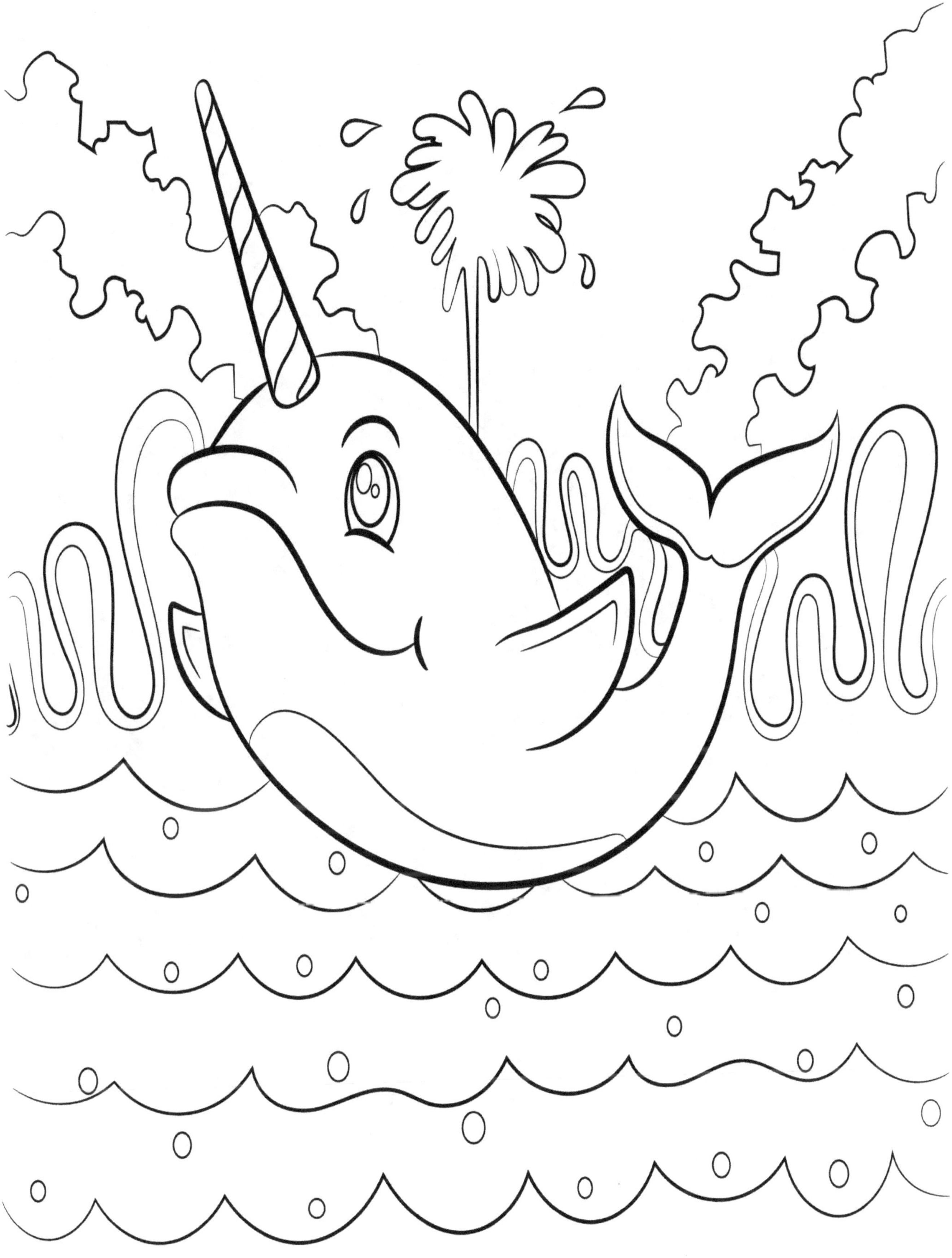

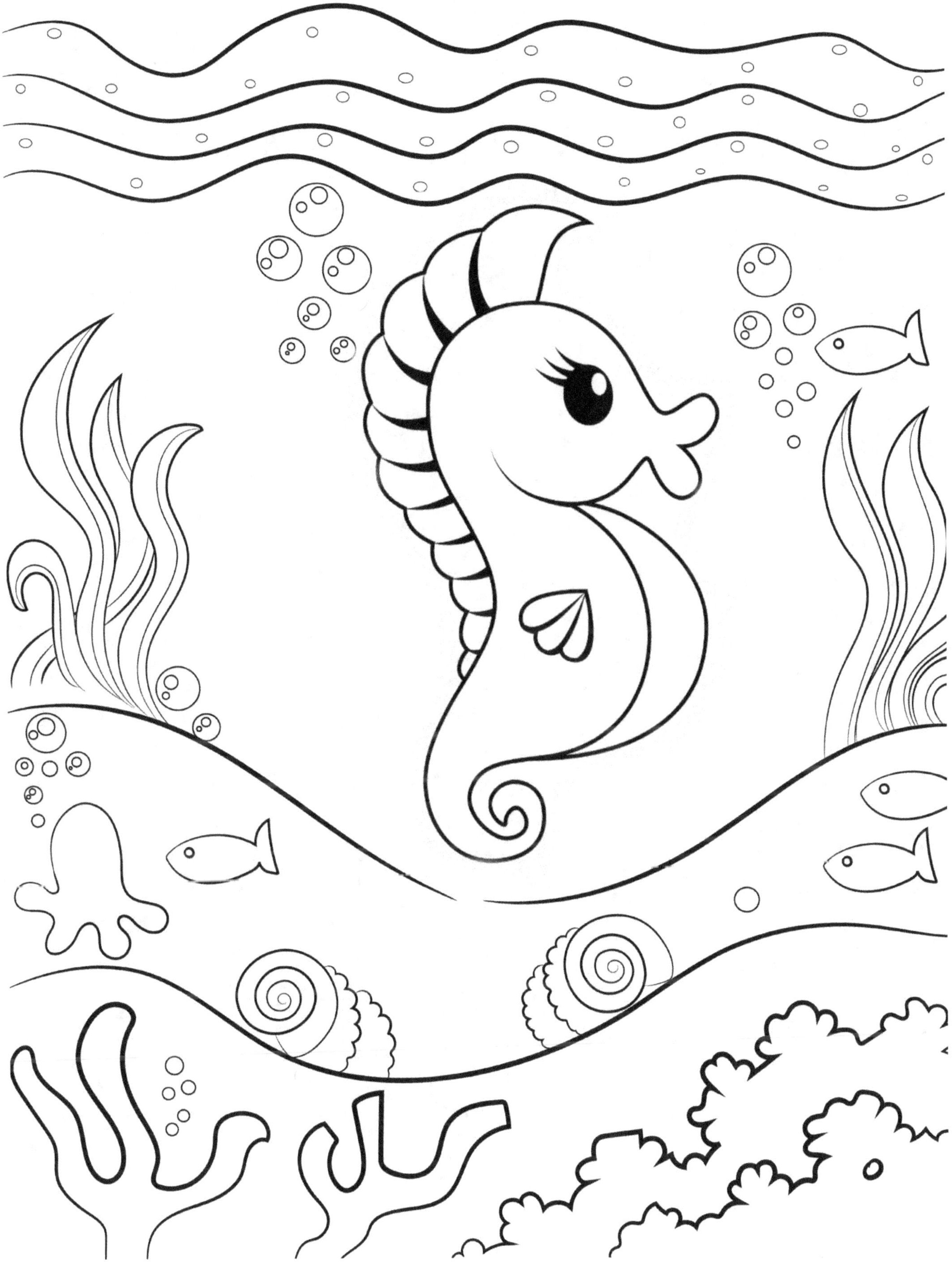

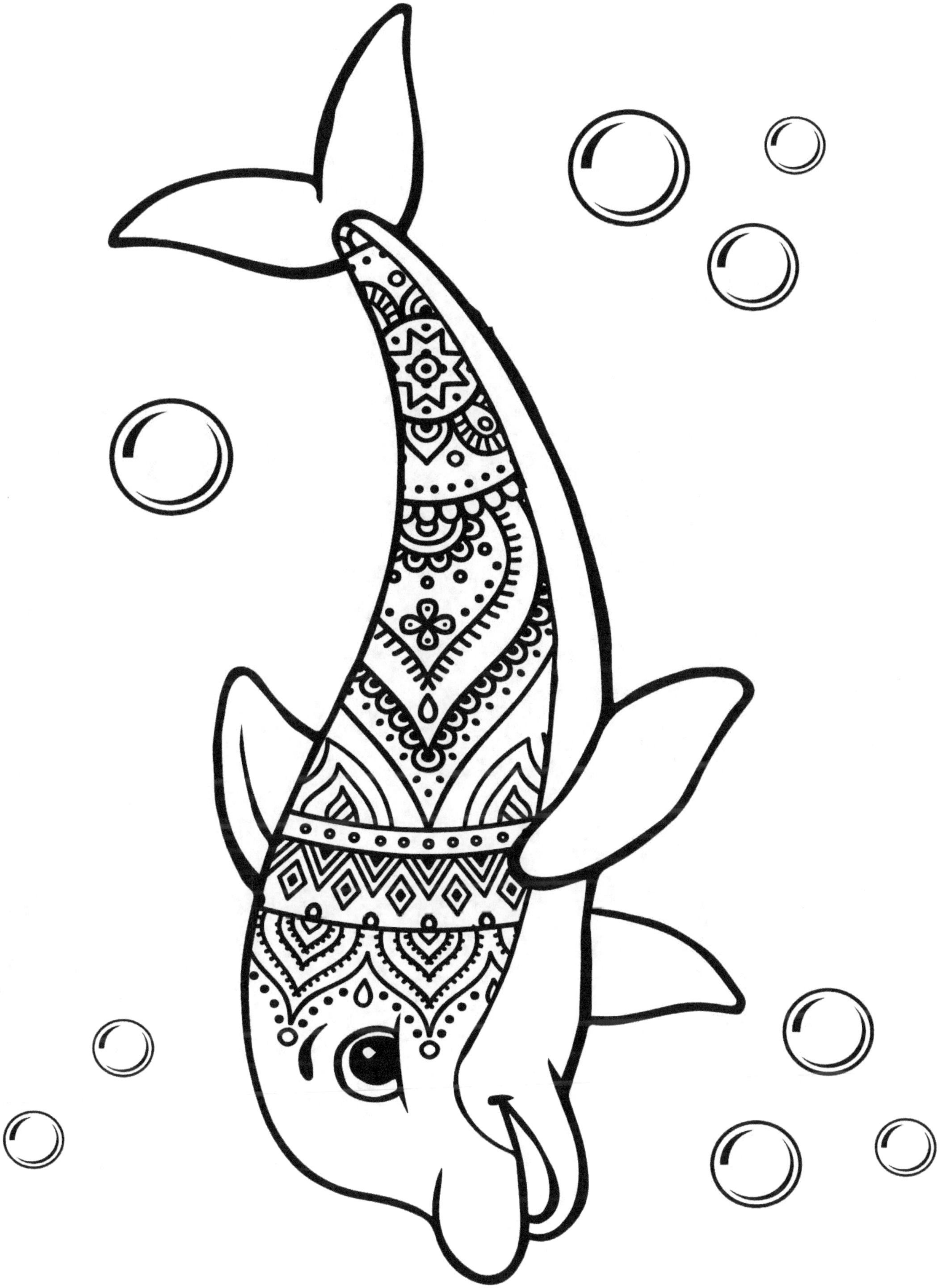

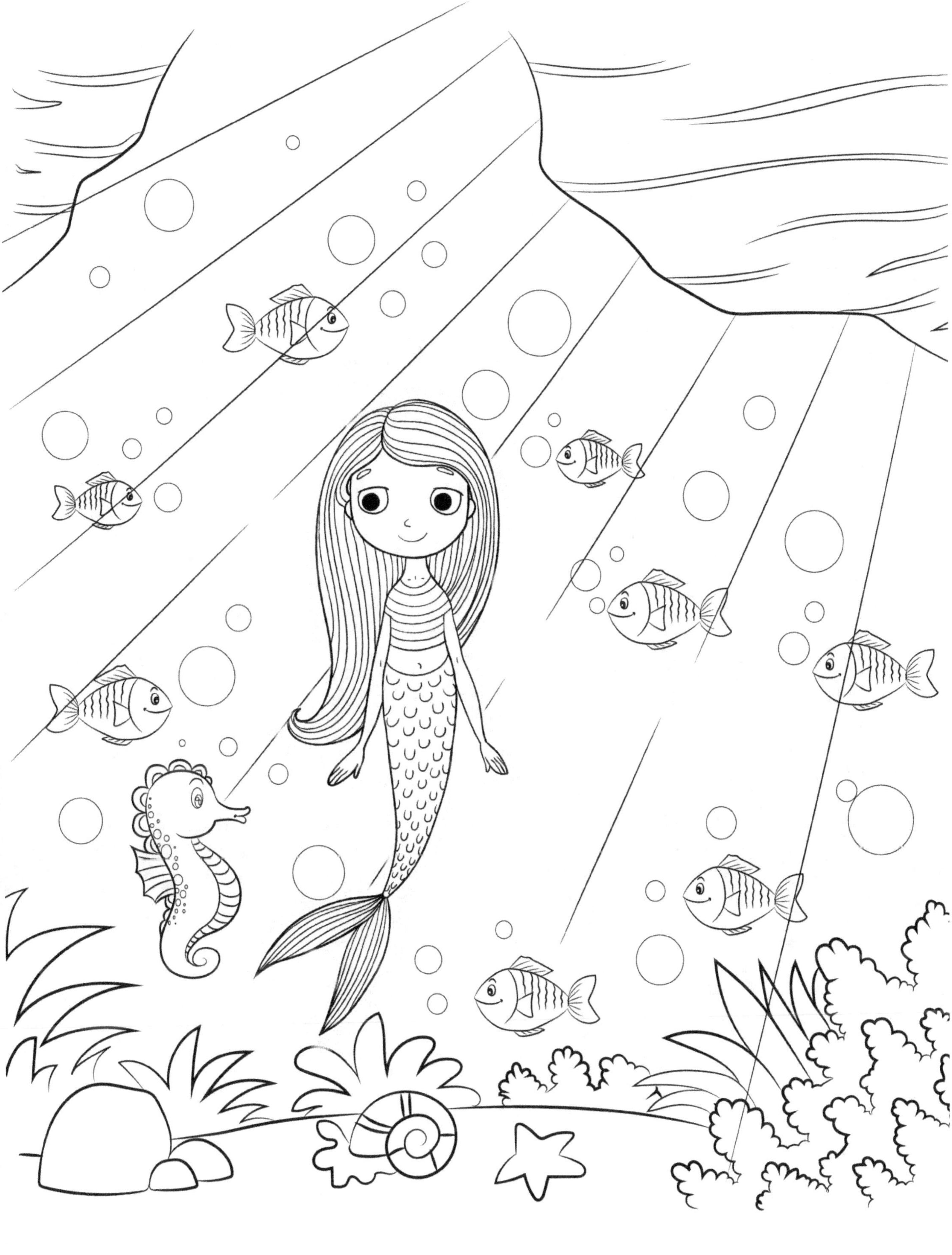

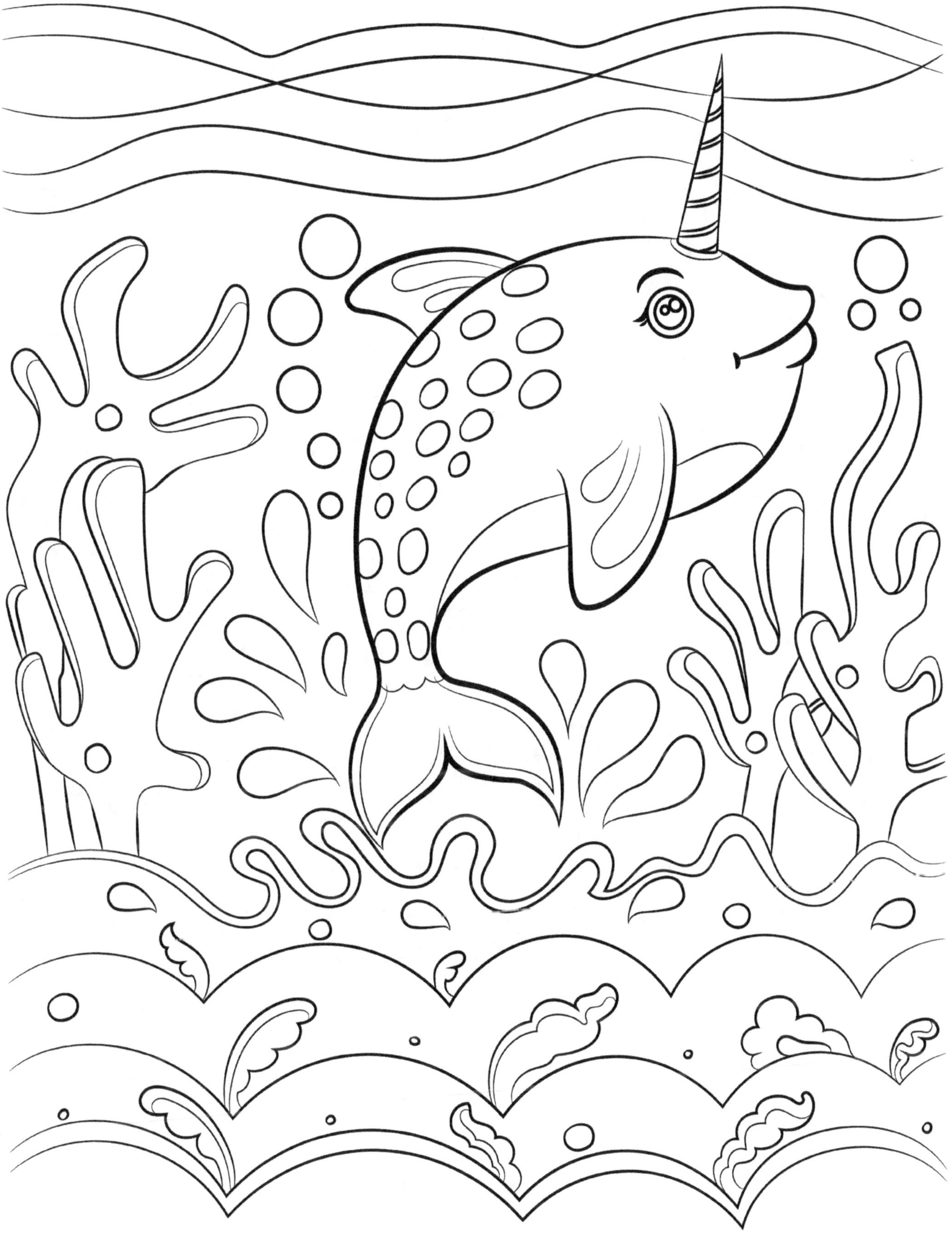

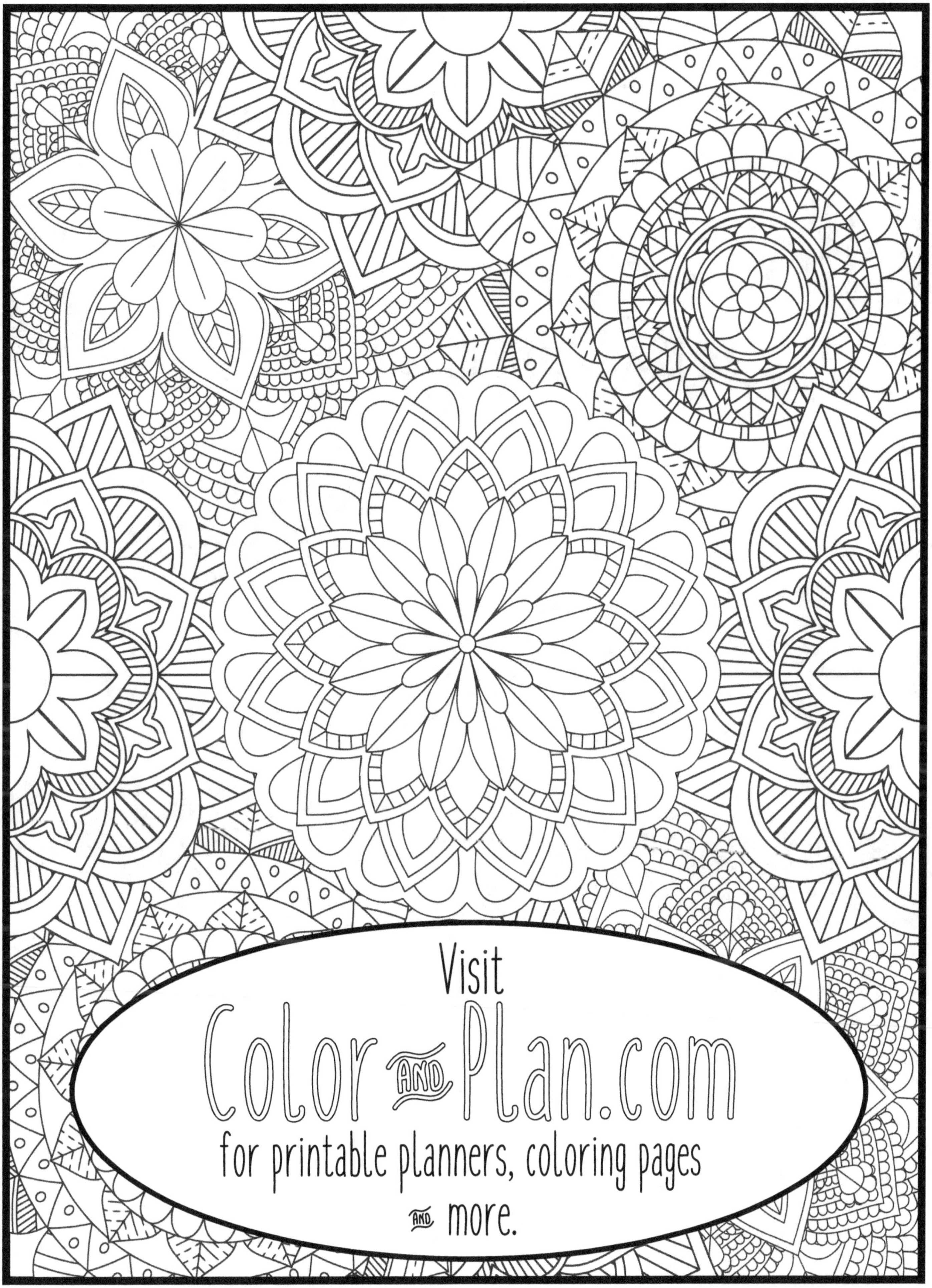
Visit
Color and Plan.com
for printable planners, coloring pages
and more.

www.ingramcontent.com/pod-product-compliance
Lightning Source LLC
Chambersburg PA
CBHW080824170526
45158CB00009B/2522